the best little whorehouse in TEXAS

SAMUEL FRENCH, INC.

45 WEST 25TH STREET	NEW YORK 10010
7623 SUNSET BOULEVARD	HOLLYWOOD 90046
LONDON	*TORONTO*

Book © 1978, 1983, by Larry L. King, Peter Masterson and Susannah Production, Ltd.

Lyrics © 1977, 1978, by Daniel Music, Ltd.; Otay Music Corp.; and MCA Music, A Division of MCA, Inc.

Amateurs wishing to arrange for the production of THE BEST LITTLE
.... plication to SAMUEL FRENCH,
.... Y. 10010, giving the following par-

.... or hall in which it is proposed to

.... the theatre or hall.

(4) The number of performances it is intended to give, and the dates thereof.

(5) The title, number of performances, gross receipts and amount of royalty and rental paid on your last musical performed.

Upon receipt of these particulars SAMUEL FRENCH, INC., will quote the amateur terms and availability.

Stock royalty and availability quoted on application to Samuel French, Inc.

For all other rights apply to The Sterling Lord Agency, Inc., 660 Madison Avenue, New York, N.Y. 10021; Ms. Susan Breitner, 1650 Broadway, New York, N.Y. 10019; The Shukat Company Ltd., 340 West 55th Street, Suite 1-A, New York, N.Y. 10019.

An orchestration consisting of a piano conductor, vocal book, country band, trumpet, trombone, reed (piccolo), violin, guitar I, guitar II, bass, and drums, will be loaned two months prior to the production ONLY on receipt of the royalty quoted for all performances, the rental fee and a refundable deposit. The deposit will be refunded on the safe return to SAMUEL FRENCH, INC. of all material loaned for the production.

Printed in U.S.A.

ISBN 0 573 69076 6

IMPORTANT ADVERTISING NOTE

All producers of THE BEST LITTLE WHOREHOUSE IN TEXAS shall announce the names of the authors. Larry L. King, Peter Masterson, and Carol Hall shall receive billing as sole authors of the Work in any and all advertising and publicity issued in connection with your production hereunder. The billing of the authors shall appear in but not be limited to all theatre programs, houseboards, throwaways, circulars, announcements, and whenever and wherever the title of the Work appears and shall be on separate lines upon which no other matter appears, immediately following the title of the Work. The names of the authors shall be in size, type and prominence at least fifty (50%) percent of the size, type and prominence of the title type or the type accorded to the names of the stars, whichever is larger. The billing shall be in the following form:

"The Best Little Whorehouse In Texas"

Book by

LARRY L. KING & PETER MASTERSON

Music & Lyrics by

CAROL HALL

(All other main credits)

Originally produced on the New York Stage
by Stevie Phillips in Association with Universal Pictures.
Originally produced by Actors Studio.

No changes, deletions or interpolations shall be made in the book, lyrics or music of the Work without the OWNERS' prior written consent.

FORTY-SIXTH STREET THEATRE

Owned and Operated by The Regency Organization, Ltd.

Irwin Meyer   Stephen R. Friedman

Universal Pictures
Presents

the best little whorehouse in

TEXAS

Book by

Larry L. King & Peter Masterson

Music & Lyrics by

Carol Hall

Musical Numbers Staged by

Tommy Tune

With

Henderson Forsythe   Carlin Glynn

Delores Hall

Jay   Pam   Clint   J. Frank   Susan   Joan
Garner   Blair   Allmon   Lucas   Mansur   Ellis

And featuring the

Rio Grande Band

Costumes by   Sets by   Musical Supervision, Direction &
                                              Lighting by   Vocal Arrangements by
Ann Roth   Marjorie Kellogg   Dennis Parichy   Robert Billig

Hair Styles by   Associate Choreographer Production Stage Manager
Michael Gottfried   Thommie Walsh   Paul Phillips

Directed by

Peter Masterson & Tommy Tune

The Producers and Theatre Management are members of
The League of New York Theatres and Producers, Inc.

CAST

(in order of appearance)

Rio Grande Band .... CRAIG CHAMBERS (BAND LEADER)

Girls .... LISA BROWN, CAROL CHAMBERS, DONNA KING,
SUSAN MANSUR, LOUISE QUICK-BOWEN, DEBRA ZALKIND

Cowboys .... JAY BURSKY, BRADLEY CLAYTON KING,
MICHAEL SCOTT, PAUL UKENA, JR.

Farmer .... CLINT ALLMON

Shy Kid .... GERRY BURKHARDT

Miss Wulla Jean .... EDNA MILTON

Traveling Salesman .... JAY GARNER

Slick Dude .... K. C. KELLY

Choir .... JAY BURSKY, BECKY GELKE, EDWINA LEWIS,
JAN MERCHANT, JAMES RICH, MARTA SANDERS

Amber .... PAMELA BLAIR

Shy .... JOAN ELLIS

Jewel .... DELORES HALL

Mona Stangley .... CARLIN GLYNN

THE GIRLS AT MISS MONA'S:
Linda Lou .... DONNA KING
Dawn .... LISA BROWN
Ginger .... LOUISE QUICK-BOWEN
Beatrice .... JAN MERCHANT
Taddy Jo .... CAROL CHAMBERS
Ruby Rae .... BECKY GELKE
Eloise .... MARTA SANDERS
Durla .... DEBRA ZALKIND

Leroy Sliney .... BRADLEY CLAYTON KING

The Dogettes .... GERRY BURKHARDT, JAY BURSKY,
MICHAEL SCOTT, PAUL UKENA, JR.

Melvin P. Thorpe .... CLINT ALLMON

Soundman .... K. C. KELLY

Stage Manager .... TOM CASHIN

Melvin Thorpe Singers .... BECKY GELKE,
BRADLEY CLAYTON KING, SUSAN MANSUR,
JAN MERCHANT, JAMES RICH, MARTA SANDERS

Sheriff Ed Earl Dodd .... HENDERSON FORSYTHE

Cameraman .... TOM CASHIN

Scruggs .... JAY GARNER

Mayor Rufus Poindexter .... J. FRANK LUCAS

Edsel Mackey .... DON CRABTREE

Doatsey Mae .... SUSAN MANSUR

Townspeople .... CAROL CHAMBERS, BRADLEY CLAYTON KING,
EDNA MILTON, JAMES RICH, MARTA SANDERS

T.V. Announcer .... LARRY L. KING

Angelette Imogene Charlene .... LISA BROWN

Angelettes .... LOUISE QUICK-BOWEN, BECKY GELKE,
DONNA KING, DEBRA ZALKIND, JAN MERCHANT

T.V. Colorman .... JAY GARNER

Senator Wingwoah .... J. FRANK LUCAS

Aggie #21 .... PAUL UKENA, JR.

Aggie #71 .... MICHAEL SCOTT

Aggie #11 .... JAY BURSKY

Ukranian Placekicker—Aggie #1 .... K. C. KELLY

Aggie #17 .... JAMES RICH

Aggie #7 .... GERRY BURKHARDT

Aggie #12—Specialty Dance .... TOM CASHIN

Aggie #77 .... BRADLEY CLAYTON KING

Photographers .... MICHAEL SCOTT, PAUL UKENA, JR.,
JAMES RICH, JAY BURSKY

Reporter #1 .... SUSAN MANSUR

Reporter #2 .... PAUL UKENA, JR.
Governor's Aide .... JAY BURSKY
Governor .... JAY GARNER
Reporter #3 .... MICHAEL SCOTT

The action takes place in the State of Texas.

THERE WILL BE ONE 12 MINUTE INTERMISSION

MUSICAL NUMBERS

ACT ONE

PROLOGUE .... Craig Chambers & The Rio Grande Band

20 FANS .... Mona, The Girls, the Cowboys, Farmer, Shy Kid,
Miss Wulla Jean, Traveling Salesman, Slick Dude and Choir

A LIL' OLE BITTY PISSANT COUNTRY PLACE . . Mona and The Girls

GIRL YOU'RE A WOMAN .... Mona, Shy, Jewel and The Girls

WATCH DOG THEME .... Melvin P. Thorpe & The Dogettes

TEXAS HAS A WHOREHOUSE IN IT .... Melvin P. Thorpe,
the Thorpe Singers & Dogettes

TWENTY-FOUR HOURS OF LOVIN' .... Jewel, The Girls

REPRISE: WATCHDOG THEME .... Dogettes

REPRISE: TEXAS HAS A WHOREHOUSE IN IT ...... Melvin P. Thorpe,
Dogettes, Mayor, Scruggs, Edsel, Doatsey Mae,
Church Lady, Lady Convent, Townspeople

DOATSEY MAE .... Doatsey Mae

ANGELETTE MARCH .... Imogene Carlene and The Angelettes

THE AGGIE SONG .... The Aggies

BUS FROM AMARILLO .... Mona

ACT TWO

THE SIDESTEP .... The Governor, Governor's Aide, Senator Wingwoah,
Melvin P. Thorpe, Dogettes, Melvin Thorpe Singers

NO LIES .... Mona, Jewel, the Girls

GOOD OLD GIRL .... The Sheriff, the Aggies

7

HARD CANDY CHRISTMAS .... Amber, Linda Lou, Ginger, Dawn, Ruby Rae, eBatrice

REPRISE: HARD CANDY CHRISTMAS .... The Girls

FINALE ....The Company

Alternate Dancers .... Monica Tiller, Jerry Yoder, and Gena Ramsel

UNDERSTUDIES

Understudies never substitute for listed players unless a specific announcement is made at the time of the performance.

For Miss Mona—Susan Mansur; for Sheriff—J. Frank Lucas; for Shy—Lisa Brown; for Doatsey—Jan Merchant; for Mayor Rufus Poindexter, Senator Wingwoah, Governor, C. J. Scruggs—Don Crabtree; for Amber, Ginger—Gena Ramsel; for Jewel—Edwina Lewis; for Edsel Mackey—Paul Ukena, Jr.; for Dawn—Monica Tiller.

LIST OF SONGS

A few minutes before curtain a GROUP OF MUSICIANS begins to drift onto the stage. THEY take their positions on the stand, beginning to tune up for the show. No lights yet. THEY should draw as little attention as possible. The tuning should really be some down home Texas music (an instrumental), beginning out of metre, then as instruments are added, picking up tempo until we are in full swing. As this opening finishes the spotlight hits the BANDLEADER.

The Best Little Whorehouse In Texas

ACT ONE

SCENE I

BANDLEADER. It was the nicest . . . little Whorehouse you ever saw. It lay about a mile down this old dirt road, and if you happened to stumble on it, you couldn't help but notice that the barns were painted and the fences were up and you might think to yourself 'why these folks would probably do to run the river with.'

(*As the music begins the stage begins to come alive, as if in the memory of the* SPEAKER. *Ceiling fans in the upstairs rooms begin to turn and we are seeing a romanticized vision of the 1930's Chicken Ranch. A warm night in the Texas country-side. The director may adjust this scene to the space available but, generally, the following occurs:*

THREE GIRLS *appear in their rooms upstairs, check their makeup and adjust their assets.* ONE *comes downstairs, ready for the evening, looking for non-existent customers. Disappointed.*)

BANDLEADER. (*Continued.*)
OH THE LITTLE HOUSE LAY
IN A GREEN TEXAS GLADE
WHERE THE TREES WERE AS COOLIN'
AS FRESH LEMONADE
THE SOFT SUMMER WIND
HAD A TRACE OF PERFUME
AND A FAN WAS TURNIN'
IN EVERY ROOM.

TWENTY FANS WERE TURNIN'
THEY WERE TURNIN'
TWENTY FANS WERE TURNIN'
IN EVERY ROOM
FEVERS WERE A BURNIN'

11

THEY WERE BURNIN'
AND THEY HAD TO HAVE
A WAY TO COOL DOWN.

(*Meanwhile a* FARMER, *in coveralls, straw hat, carrying a burlap bag, enters, smiles gleefully, sneaks up on her and grabs her from behind in a playful embrace.* SHE *is spooked, but sees* HE's *a friend and* THEY *sit down together.*)

BANDLEADER. (*Continued.*) Since the 1890's this has been one of the better pleasure palaces in all Texas. In fact, they say that some of our Lanville County boys celebrated here before going off to fight with Teddy Roosevelt at San Juan Hill.

(*A* SHY KID *gawks into the room, obviously for his first visit.* HE *is gazing around like a hick in the city, at the same time holding a wad of dollar bills. As his gaze lands on the* FIRST GIRL *and the* FARMER *his mouth drops open and his money floats to the floor.* HE *recovers and quickly falls to his knees and picks it up.*

GIRL 2 *has come down and appears behind* SHY KID, *scaring him.* SHE *calms him and sits with him, beginning work on him quietly.*

GIRL 3 *appears, looking provocative and holding a fan over her mouth, slinks by the farmer, who notices, but* GIRL 1 *grabs him and takes him up to ther room.* — UP CENTER. HE *leers back at* GIRL 3 *but clutching his burlap bag.*)

BANDLEADER. (*Continued.*) At first it was right on Main Street, up above the hardware store. But about 1915 some of the local Jesus bunch got on their high horses and the girls moved out of the city limits, just past the "Bad Curve" sign.

(MISS WULLA JEAN *is pushed on in a wheel chair and makes a grand tour of the room, stopping to talk to* GIRL 2. *As* SHE *is distracted,* GIRL 3 *slips over and whispers something shocking, but not unpleasant to the shy kid.* GIRL 2 *turns back, catching her and tells her off in no uncertain terms.* GIRL 4 *retreats with her fan to the steps.*)

BANDLEADER. (*Continued.*) It was during the Hoover depression that Miss Wulla Jean come along. She put in a set of rules just a shade less rigid than the ten commandments. You see, Miss Wulla Jean didn't appreciate perversions. So, she cut out all the exotic extras. But she did like for her ladies, as she called them, to treat her customers real nice.

(*A* TRAVELING SALESMAN *rushes onto the stage and looks around hungrily.* HE *sees* GIRL 3, *looking beautiful and makes an approach.* HE *tells her a quick joke,* SHE *laughs, exposes her mouth. No teeth.* HE *grimaces.* GIRL 4 *is conveniently there to ask him to dance and* HE *goes with her.*)

"20 FANS"

BANDLEADER. (*Continued.*)
IT HAD NICE WATERMELONS
ALL COVERED WITH VINES
AND A VEGETABLE GARDEN
A FEW SLENDER PINES
WHITE PAINTED FENCE
WITH THE ROSES IN BLOOM
AND A FAN WAS TURNIN'
IN EVERY ROOM.
She put a jukebox in the parlor to sorta help break the ice. A feller could ask a girl for a dance, or if he held back a little, she'd ask him. And pretty soon they'd get a little business on. Three dollars worth. You see, that was back in the old days . . . when Roosevelt nooky was cheaper than Carter coffee.

(SLICK DUDE *enters. The* SLICK DUDE *swaggers into the Center of the room.* HE *sees himself as Rudolph Valentino, Marlon Brando, or probably Elvis since this is rural.* HE *looks around, focuses on* GIRL 2, *who is beside him. Does a sleight of hand and takes a cigarette from behind her ear.* SHE *giggles.* HE *strikes a kitchen match on his fly, lights up and holds the match for her to blow out. The* SHY KID *is watching and* SLICK DUDE *hands him the hot match, which* HE *takes, and reacts in pain as Slick Dude swaggers over to the juke box.*)

BANDLEADER. (*Continued.*)
WHEN THE SUN WOULD GO DOWN
IN A WILD BLAZE OF LIGHT
THEN THE LITTLE HOUSE LAY
IN THE STILLNESS OF NIGHT

FIREFLIES WOULD FLICKER
AND FLOAT IN THE GLOOM
WHILE A FAN WAS TURNIN'
IN EVERY ROOM

(EVERYONE *Onstage freezes. We hear the* CHOIR *in the distance and approaching. Then* THEY *appear, saint-like, in robes, as if* THEY *were in another part of town.*)

CHOIR.
TWENTY FANS WERE TURNIN'
THEY WERE TURNIN'
TWENTY FANS WERE TURNIN'
IN EVERY ROOM
FEVERS WERE A BURNIN'
THEY WERE BURNIN'
AND THEY HAD TO HAVE
A WAY TO COOL DOWN.

(MISS WULLA JEAN *sees* GIRL 3 *exposing her legs to the* SHY KID *and signals to be pushed over to confront and correct her.* SHE *shakes her cane at her and signals to be pushed Offstage.*)

BANDLEADER. Miss Wulla Jean had a strict rule against competing for customers. And if she caught one of the girls flashing her wares a little more than she thought was ladylike, she raised nine kinds of hell. And she insisted that each girl check her customer real good for the clap and wash him off with soap and warm water. Some of the fellas claimed that was the best part.

(*In the upstairs room behind venetian blinds,* GIRL 1 *is washing the* FARMER's *privates in a hand basin. His back is to the audience and* HE *is wearing long johns as well as his straw hat. When* SHE *has finished her task,* HE *grabs her from behind.*)

BANDLEADER. (*Continued.*) But you didn't have to worry about catchin' nothin' here like you did with them freelancin' girls down in Galveston.

(SHE *pushes him away.*)

GIRL 1. Now I told you honey, I gotta have my three dollars first. Miss Wulla Jean don't allow no honeyfuggin' till I pay my rent.

(*The* FARMER *picks up a bag* HE *has carefully brought along.*)

BANDLEADER. It wasn't always easy to come up with three dollars. Especially during the hard times.

(*The* FARMER *pulls a chicken out of the bag and holds it out proudly to barter.* HE *breaks into a mock chicken sound as* HE *presents it.*)

FARMER.
POC, POC, POC, POC.

(GIRL 1 *looks disgusted.*)

GIRL 1. Well you just keep the chickens in the bag and I'll take them out back soon as you're finished. (GIRL 1 *goes about her job with resolution, embraces him.* HE *turns her around,* SHE *understands.*)

BANDLEADER. And so the girls began accepting poultry in trade. And that's how the place got its name, The Chicken Ranch. And if you grew up anywhere in Texas, you knew at an early age that they were selling something out there other than *pullets.*

(*As the tempo picks up, the* FARMER *lifts her onto his thighs and* THEY *rock together in tempo.* SHE *rides him not unlike a circus girl riding a pony.*

The SHY KID *dumps* GIRL 2, *grabs* GIRL 3 *and* THEY *go upstairs together.*

GIRL 2, *disgusted, makes a pass at* SLICK DUDE. *But* GIRL 5 *arrives late and* HE *immediately goes for her, takes off his belt and pops her playfully from behind as* THEY *go to her room.*

The Traveling Salesman and GIRL 4 *are still dancing.*)

CHOIR & COWBOYS & BANDLEADER.
TWENTY FANS WERE TURNIN'
THEY WERE TURNIN'
TWENTY FANS WERE TURNIN'
IN EVERY ROOM
FEVERS WERE A BURNIN'
THEY WERE BURNIN'
AND THEY HAD TO HAVE
A WAY TO COOL DOWN.

(GIRL 1 *falls forward on her hands, the* FARMER *still between her skyward legs as* HE *continues.*)

CHOIR & COWBOYS & BANDLEADER (*Continued.*)
TWENTY FANS WERE HUMMIN'
THEY WERE HUMMIN'
TWENTY FANS WERE HUMMIN'
IN EVERY ROOM
CUSTOMERS WERE COMIN'
THEY WERE COMIN'
AND THEY HAD TO HAVE A
WAY TO COOL DOWN.

(EVERYONE *listens to the* FARMER*'s cry.*)

FARMER.	CHOIR.
I'M COMIN'! I'M COMIN'! THANK YOU, THANK YOU, JESUS!	AHHHHHHHHH

(*The* FARMER *gets dressed,* GIRL 1 *tidies herself up and is getting him out quickly.*

GIRL 2 *tries to horn in on* TRAVELING SALESMAN, HE *being the only male left unoccupied. No dice.* HE *dances* GIRL 4 *up to her room.*

GIRL 2 *stomps off in anger.*

The rooms are alive with activity which is stylized but suggestive of sexual behavior.

The FARMER *is about to leave the house with the chicken in the burlap bag.*

GIRL 1 *calls him back.* HE *takes out the chicken, holding it on high and presents it* CENTER STAGE. SHE *takes it.*)

CHOIR, COWBOYS, BANDLEADER.
TWENTY FANS WERE TURNIN'
THEY WERE TURNIN'
TWENTY FANS WERE TURNIN'
IN EVERY ROOM
FEVERS WERE A BURNIN'
THEY WERE BURNIN'
AND THEY HAD TO HAVE A
WAY TO COOL DOWN.

TWENTY FANS WERE HUMMIN'
THEY WERE HUMMIN'
TWENTY FANS WERE HUMMIN'
IN EVERY ROOM
CUSTOMERS WERE COMIN'
THEY WERE COMIN'
AND THEY HAD TO HAVE
A WAY TO COOL DOWN.

(*Everything freezes except* FARMER *and* GIRL 1)

GIRL 1. Y'all come back now, ya hear.

(*The* BAND *ends song as* GIRL 1 *exits with chicken.*

Blackout. The faint light Center and Spot on BANDLEADER.

A GIRL *pushes the empty wheelchair slowly to center and leaves it there in the half light.*)

BANDLEADER. Well, that was in the old days. But about ten years ago, Miss Wulla Jean died. She bequeathed the place in her will to her favorite working girl, Mona Stangley, who you might say had worked her way up from the bottom. Mona pretty well carried out the old traditions of The Chicken Ranch. And that's probably why they lived in peace with the town for so long. That is, until about a year ago, Thanksgiving . . .

ACT ONE

SCENE 2

Two girls, ANGEL *and* SHY, *walk up to the porch of the Chicken Ranch.* ANGEL *is the most obvious-looking whore you'll see all night.* SHE *has a wild hairdo, and city whore clothes, bright makeup, the works.* SHE *wears dark glasses.* SHY *is the opposite. A country girl, young, fresh off the farm, maybe even gawky.* SHY *hesitates outside the place.*

ANGEL. You don't have to worry about nothin'. Just let me do th' talkin'. And try not to act like you just rode in on a load of turkeys.

SHY. I'm scared.

ANGEL. Well, take off then. Nobody's holdin' a gun to your head.

SHY. I know it. (ANGEL *checks her makeup in a hand mirror, lifts her glasses exposing a black eye.*)

ANGEL. I shoulda just let you find your own way out here. (SHY *nods.*)

ANGEL. (*Continued.*) Out of all them people on the bus how come you to ask *me* where this place was at?

SHY. You just looked like you might know.

ANGEL. Thanks a lot! Takes one to know one! Come on, follow me. (*Angel wiggles sexily into the parlor of the Chicken Ranch.* SHY *strides in behind her like* SHE *is following a plow, and hangs by the front door, not sure whether* SHE *wants to be there or not.*)

ANGEL. (*Continued.*) Hello! Is the Madam here?

(JEWEL, *an older black woman, comes out of the kitchen.* SHE *eyes* ANGEL.)

JEWEL. She ever hear you call her "Madam" and you won't stay here. She got more pride than the U.S. Marines. We calls her "Miss Mona."

ANGEL. Well, okay. Can we see her?

JEWEL I don't suppose you want to sell her no Tupperware. (SHE *laughs uproariously at her own joke.*) Hold on a minute, honey, I'll get her. (*Calling.*) Miss Mona, there some girls down here to see you.

Miss Mona. All right, Jewel, I'll be right down.

(Angel *wiggles over to the* Stage Left *stairs and perches herself, showing a knee. In other words, showing her wares for the interview.*

Shy *takes a pickup truck rear view mirror out of her brown paper sack and checks her appearance, maybe pinching her cheeks for color.*

Mona *enters at the head of the stairs beautifully coiffed like Tammy Wynette and outfitted in a theatrical lounging costume.*)

Miss Mona. (*Continued.*) Well now . . . What happened? Did the Texas Rangers raid Galveston again. (She *notices* Shy *standing by the door.*) Or was it a hurricane? I never had girls linin' up for jobs before.

Angel. Are you hirin' on anybody?

Miss Mona. Maybe. And maybe not. I'm kind of choosy about who lives in this house. Right, Jewel?

Jewel. Yes, M'am.

(Mona *crosses to* Angel, *takes off the dark glasses, exposing black eye.*)

Miss Mona. Pimp whup up on you, honey?

Angel. I wadn't holdin' out on him!

Miss Mona. Uh huh! (*To* Shy.) Honey, you comin' or goin'?

Shy. Yes, M'am. I mean I'm comin'.

Miss Mona. Then why don't you take a seat?

Shy. Yes, M'am. (She *shuffles over to the* Stage Right *stair and sits.*)

Miss Mona. (*Sitting in wheel chair,* Center.) So. How much experience have you all had?

Angel. Amateur or professional? Ha, ha!

Miss Mona. For money, hunny!

Angel. (*Sobering.*) About four years.

Miss Mona. (*To* Shy.) How about you?

Shy. None.

Miss Mona. None, huh? Well, Thursday I'm gonna have a whole house full of college boys and they probably hadn't had none either.

ANGEL. College boys?

MISS MONA. Yeah, the winning seniors from the Texas Aggie-Texas U team gets treated to a night here on Thanksgiving by their Alumni Association.

ANGEL. That sounds like fun.

MISS MONA. It's bad for a workin' girl to get to enjoying it too much.

ANGEL. The Johns usually see to it that I don't.

MISS MONA. Hunny! We don't call 'em "Johns" here. We don't call 'em "Tricks." Not even "Customers," no we call 'em . . . Guests.

ANGEL. Guests?

MISS MONA. Guests. We make 'em feel at home, without makin' 'em feel at home, if you get what I mean.

ANGEL. (*Grinning.*) I think I do. Well, to tell the truth. I'm sick of workin' spots all over the state. Movin' all the time from Hotel to Motel. Pimps beatin' you up, takin' your money, bellboys makin' you give 'em free pussy.

MISS MONA. Now hold it right there. I don't allow my girls to talk like that. Couldn't you just say "free samples?"

ANGEL. (*A bit dubious.*) Yes, M'am. Anyway, I couldn't save any money, and these pimps . . . these uh . . . sample salesmen?

MISS MONA. Now that's very ladylike.

ANGEL. Anyhow, they took my money and they beat my ass . . . my person, and half the time when I did get busted they wouldn't even be around to bail me out.

MISS MONA. I don't want nobody around here who's got law troubles. They after you for anything?

ANGEL. Aw, no, M'am! I'm clean as a whistle! (SHE *whistles. Looks as innocent as possible.* MISS MONA *stares at her steadily.*)

MISS MONA. How many times you been vagged for prostitution?

ANGEL. Not many.

MISS MONA. *How* many?

ANGEL. Maybe . . . six? Prob'ly not even that many.

MISS MONA. Hot checks?

ANGEL. No.

MISS MONA. Assault?

ANGEL. None of that. (MONA *checks her neck.*)

MISS MONA. Clawin' and scratchin'?

ANGEL. I told you everything.

Miss Mona. You dope? You got a habit? (Miss Mona *checks her arms for marks.*)

Angel. No, M'am!

Miss Mona. Don't even like nose candy?

Angel. Like *what*?

Miss Mona. (*With knowing smile.*) Cocaine, Hunny.

Angel. I don't fool with that stuff!

Miss Mona. Speed?

Angel. No!

Miss Mona. Grass?

Angel. Well, I have experimented with grass.

Miss Mona. (*Sternly.*) From now on leave the experiments to science. I'll crack down on doping in a New York minute. (Mona *turns toward* Shy, *who extends her arms for inspection.*) That's all right, Honey. I think maybe I'd better lay down the rules of my place before I do any hirin'. You see this is a country house. It ain't no city place. We get a different kind of customer here. We get local businessmen, Bohemian farmers, Congressmen from over at Austin. Now we used to get a bunch of roughnecks when the oil wells was pumpin' but thank God the field dried up, pay day got a little too rambunctious. No, mainly we get a nice quiet group and I aim to keep it that way.

"A LIL' OLE BITTY PISSANT COUNTRY PLACE"

IT'S JUST A LITTLE BITTY PISSANT COUNTRY PLACE
NOTHIN' MUCH TO SEE
NO DRINKIN' ALLOWED
WE GET A NICE QUIET CROWD
PLAIN AS IT CAN BE.

IT'S JUST A PIDDLY SQUATTIN' OLE TIME COUNTRY
PLACE
NOTHIN' TOO HIGH TONED
JES LOTS OF GOOD WILL
AND MAYBE ONE SMALL THRILL
BUT THERE'S NOTHIN' DIRTY GOING ON!

Band.
NOTHIN' DIRTY GOIN' ON.

Miss Mona.
I DON'T HIRE NO MARRIED GIRLS
THEY'RE NOT ON THE BALL

THEY GOT HOMES AND HUSBANDS
THEY'RE NOT STABLE AT ALL.
THEY DON'T UNDERSTAND A SINGLE THING
ABOUT A PROPER BUSINESS DAY
NOW WHAT'S THE POINT OF OPENIN' UP THE STORE
IF YOU GIVE THE GOODS AWAY?

   Miss Mona and Band.

IT'S JUST A LITTLE BITTY PISSANT COUNTRY PLACE
NOTHIN' MUCH TO SEE
NO DRINKIN' ALLOWED
WE GET A NICE QUIET CROWD
PLAIN AS IT CAN BE.

IT'S JUST A PIDDLY SQUATTIN' OLE TIME COUNTRY
PLACE
NOTHIN' TOO HIGH TONED
JES LOTS OF GOOD WILL
AND MAYBE ONE SMALL THRILL
BUT THERE'S NOTHIN' DIRTY GOIN' ON!

   Miss Mona.

KEEP YOUR LANGUAGE CLEAN, GIRL
KEEP YOUR BEDROOM NEAT
DON'T HANG AROUND THE TOWN CAFE
OR SAY HI' ON THE STREET.
AND IF YOU MIND YOUR P'S AND Q'S AND MANNERS
YOU DON'T NEED NO OTHER TOOLS
BUT BEFORE I FINISH I SHOULD ADD
MY SPECIAL NO NO RULES.

   Band.

MISS MONA'S GONNA LAY IT DOWN
HER SPECIAL NO NO RULES

   Miss Mona.

BEDS ARE NOT TO BE WALLOWED IN
THAT'S THE KIND OF THING
THAT BIG FAT LAZY HOGS DO
(AND IT DON'T MAKE MONEY)

AND I WON'T TOLERATE NO TYIN'
UP MY TELEPHONE WITH OTHER
PEOPLE'S BUSINESS
(ARE YOU WITH ME, HONEY)

AND PLEASE DON'T SHOW ME
NO TATTOOS, NO HEARTS AND FLOWERS
ON YOUR THIGH
(IT'S DOWNRIGHT TACKY)

BRANDS BELONG ON CATTLE
AND THAT AIN'T WHAT WE'RE
SELLIN' AT MISS MONA'S
(DO YOU CATCH MY DRIFT?)

I PAY THE FOOD AND THE RENT AND THE UTILITIES
YOU KEEP YOUR MIND ON YOUR WORK
RESPONSIBILITIES
DON'T LET YOUR MOUTH OVERLOAD YOUR
CAPABILITIES
AND WE CAN GET ALONG.

AND AS FOR PIMPS, PIMPS ARE SOMETHIN'
YOU DON'T NEED TO GET YOUR DAILY BUSINESS
DONE
(ARE YOU LISTENIN' GOOD)
SO KEEP THOSE LEECHES AND BLOODSUCKERS OFF
THE BACKROAD
I KNOW HOW TO USE A GUN
(NO ONE MESSES WITH MY GIRLS)

AND ANY QUESTIONS YOU MIGHT HAVE
ABOUT THE WAY I RUN THIS PLACE
DON'T GRIPE AND WHINE
BEHIND MY BACK
JUST TELL ME FACE TO FACE
I'M OPEN-MINDED
SAY IT ALL
THEN GO UPSTAIRS AND PACK
(THE DOOR'S THAT WAY)
  Miss Mona and Bandleader.
I PAY THE FOOD AND THE RENT AND THE UTILITIES
YOU KEEP YOUR MIND ON YOUR WORK
RESPONSIBILITIES
DON'T LET YOUR MOUTH OVERLOAD YOUR
CAPABILITIES

Miss Mona.
AND WE CAN GET ALONG.

ANY BAD HABITS YOU COME IN WITH
GET RID OF RIGHT NOW
I CAIN'T STAND NO CHEWIN' GUM
IT LOOKS JUST LIKE A COW.

ANYONE TAKIN' SICK LEAVE
OUGHTA BE REAL SURE THEY'RE SICK
AND EVERY TIME YOU HEAR THIS BELL
BETTER GET HERE DOUBLE QUICK.

(Mona *rings a bell and the* Girls *appear from everywhere, in various stages of half-dress.*)

Miss Mona. (*Continued.*) All my girls know the rules by heart. Linda Lou, start 'em.

Linda Lou. No whips or rough stuff, this ain't the Marine Corps. No three or more in a bed, this ain't the circus. And no kissin' on the mouth, this ain't the Junior prom, Ruby Rae . . .

Ruby Rae.
BEDS ARE NOT TO BE WALLOWED IN
THAT'S THE KIND OF THING
THAT BIG FAT LAZY HOGS DO
(AND IT DON'T MAKE MONEY), BEATRICE . . .

Beatrice.
AND I WON'T TOLERATE NO TYIN'
UP MY TELEPHONE WITH OTHER
PEOPLE'S BUSINESS . . . ELOISE HONEY . . .

Eloise.
AND PLEASE DON'T SHOW ME
NO TATTOOS, NO HEARTS AND FLOWERS
ON YOUR THIGH

Durla.
IT'S DOWNRIGHT TACKY

All.
BRANDS BELONG ON CATTLE
AND THAT AIN'T WHAT WE'RE
SELLING AT MISS MONA'S

Eloise.
DO YOU CATCH MY DRIFT?

ALL GIRLS.
I PAY THE FOOD AND THE RENT AND THE UTILITIES
YOU KEEP YOUR MIND ON YOUR WORK
RESPONSIBILITIES
DON'T LET YOUR MOUTH OVERLOAD YOUR
CAPABILITIES
  MISS MONA.
AND WE CAN GET ALONG . . . DAWN . . .
  DAWN.
ANY BAD HABITS YOU COME IN WITH
GET RID OF RIGHT NOW
  MISS MONA.
TADDY JO . . .
  TADDY JO.
I CAN'T STAND NO CHEWIN' GUM
IT LOOKS JUS' LIKE A COW.
  MISS MONA.
DURLA . . .
  DURLA.
ANYONE TAKIN' SICK LEAVE
OUGHTA BE REAL SURE THEY'RE SICK
  MISS MONA.
GINGER!
  GINGER.
EVERYTIME YOU HEAR THIS BELL
BETTER GET HERE DOUBLE QUICK.

(GIRLS *ad lib*)

  GIRLS.
IT'S JUST A LITTLE BITTY PISSANT COUNTRY PLACE
NOTHIN' MUCH TO SEE
NO DRINKIN' ALLOWED
WE GET A NICE QUIET CROWD
PLAIN AS IT CAN BE.

IT'S JUST A PIDDLY SQUATTIN' OLD TIME COUNTRY
PLACE
NOTHIN' TOO HIGH TONED
JES LOTS OF GOOD WILL
AND MAYBE ONE SMALL THRILL
BUT THERE'S NOTHIN' DIRTY GOIN' ON.

IT'S JUST A LITTLE BITTY PISSANT COUNTRY PLACE
NOTHIN' MUCH TO SEE
NO DRINKIN' ALLOWED
WE GET A NICE QUIET CROWD
PLAIN AS IT CAN BE.

IT'S JUST A PIDDLY SQUATTIN' OLD TIME COUNTRY
PLACE
NOTHIN' TOO HIGH TONED
JES LOTS OF GOOD WILL
AND MAYBE ONE SMALL THRILL
BUT THERE'S NOTHIN' DIRTY GOIN' ON

NOTHIN' DIRTY GOIN' ON.

Miss Mona. There is one more rule. If I ever find you in bed with any of the other girls, I'll be quick to hand you a sandwich and a roadmap.

Angel. I'm not like that!

Miss Mona. Yeah, that's what they all say. You got a problem with that particular rule?

Angel. I most certainly do not.

Miss Mona. How 'bout you? (They *all look at* Shy.)

Shy. I don't even know what you all are talkin' about.

Miss Mona. Good! Lord girls, I plumb forgot my manners. What're your names?

Angel. Nancy Jean Drury.

Miss Mona. Is that your workin' name?

Angel. Oh, no, M'am. I've worked as Sadie, as Marsha, as Sheila, Queen of the jungle . . . well, I've been called more names than a baseball umpire.

Miss Mona. Well, hunny, you know what I think? I think if you would take this Dolly Parton dead sheep off your head . . . (Mona *takes the wig off* Angel, *exposing her ratty looking hair.* Angel *ducks her head in shock and shame.*)

Miss Mona. (*Continued.*) C'mon, hunny, let me see your face . . . and maybe scrub off some of that pancake makeup, why you would be a lot like the girl next door type . . . Innocent. Now, I would call you Dawn, but I got me a Dawn.

Dawn. Howdy.

Angel. I've thought about . . . Angel.

(*The* Girls *all laugh.*)

MISS MONA. Angel! . . . Well now, that is a right pretty name. Okay then . . . Angel.

ANGEL. Can I stay on then?

MISS MONA. Well, I'm gonna try you out for a while.

SHY. Yee Haw!

MISS MONA. (MONA *turns to* SHY.) Okay, hunny, what's your name?

SHY. Annamerle Seltzer.

MISS MONA. Annamerle Seltzer. Good God, it sounds like a headache powder!

SHY. I don't think it's no worse than Modene Gunch and I went to school with her!

MISS MONA. Now don't go getting your feelin's hurt, hunny. It's just that it ain't easy sellin' Annamerle Seltzer, even at our reduced rates. No, I'm just gona call you Shy, til I can think of somethin' better.

ANGEL. How much do you charge for . . . What do you call it?

GINGER. We try not to call it!

MISS MONA. We keep it reasonable.

GINGER. Fifteen for a straight date, with a twenty minute time limit.

BEATRICE. And twenty for half an' half.

DAWN. And twenty five for French.

MISS MONA. You ladies do speak a certain kind of French, don't you?

ANGEL. Fluently.

SHY. I thought you said you didn't allow no kissin' on the mouth?

MISS MONA. Shy, hunny, I think that you and me are gonna have to have a little private talk.

ANGEL. What's the workin' hours?

GINGER. A week of day duty, a week of night duty.

LINDA LOU. You work six days a week here, sweetheart, except when you got the curse.

MISS MONA. And when you got the curse you may leave this house for up to three days.

BEATRICE. But don't try gettin' it more than once a month.

ANGEL. Well, the prices seem a little . . .

MISS MONA. Low? Well, you gotta look at it this way, hunny. We go in for mass volume and repeat business . . . just like Coca Cola and McDonald's hamburgers. Besides, you are not

gonna have the usual overhead here. (MONA *signals to the band and sings.*)
YOU DON'T GET NO FINES, GIRL . . .
    GIRLS.
YOU DON'T PAY NO BAIL
    MISS MONA.
YOU DON'T SPEND NO TIME, GIRL
SITTIN' IN THE JAIL
    GIRLS.
SO YOU CAN SEE THAT IT'S A BIG ADVANTAGE
IF MISS MONA IS THE BOSS
    MISS MONA.
I GOT ONLY ONE MORE THING TO SAY
THERE'S A GROUP RATE ON BLUE CROSS
    ANGEL. When do we start?
    MISS MONA. You can go on the night shift. I'm not finished with Shy here. Ruby Rae show Angel to her room. And hunny, you better git some rest. Friday's payday at the cotton gin and it's gonna be a long night.
    RUBY RAE. Come on, Angel.

(*The* GIRLS ALL *sing the following verse as* THEY *go off to their rooms leaving* MISS MONA *and* SHY *alone on the stage.*)

    GIRLS.
IT'S JUST A PIDDLY SQUATTIN' OLD TIME COUNTRY PLACE
NOTHIN' TOO HIGH TONED
JES LOTS OF GOOD WILL
AND MAYBE ONE SMALL THRILL
BUT THERE'S NOTHIN' DIRTY GOIN' ON.

(ALL *freeze except* MONA *and* SHY.)

ACT ONE

SCENE 3

SHY *drapes herself on the stairs as sexily as possible.*

    MISS MONA. What are you doin' here, hunny?

(SHY *is near tears and* SHE *shakes her head in a cross between bewilderment and emotion.*)

MISS MONA. (*Continued.*) I think maybe you better just head on back home.

SHY. I'm broke.

MISS MONA. Well, I could lend you fifty dollars. Course you'd have to pay me back someday.

SHY. It ain't that, m'am. I got nowheres to go home to.

MISS MONA. Boyfriend treat you bad?

SHY. No, M'am.

MISS MONA. Folks run you off?

SHY. No, but I ain't never goin' back there. (SHE *glares straight at* MONA *and we see a toughness for the first time.*)

MISS MONA. Did your Daddy get sweet on you, hunny?

(SHY*'s head goes down to her lap again.* SHE *can't answer, but we know it's true.*)

MISS MONA. (*Continued.*) Well, that ain't the first time it's happened to a girl, it ain't gonna be the last. Men ain't all bad, they're just 92% bad. Maybe I can get you on as a waitress over at the cafe.

SHY. No. I don't want no waitressin' job! I done thought about this. I'm gonna stay right here . . . I mean if you'll let me.

MIS MONA. Well now, you are gonna take a lot of fixin'. I reckon those are your good clothes.

SHY. Yes, M'am.

MISS MONA. Jewel can take you over to Austin tomorrow. You see, hunny, my girls dress real nice. Men like that. The day shift wears sort of slinky sports outfits and the night shift wears long dresses. You can pay me back out of your first earnings. If I can get you in at the beauty parlor this afternoon you can be ready to start tomorrow. That's about the only sit down place you can go in town, and then only the back two stations. Hell, I was gonna put my own in out here, but the Chamber of Commerce bitched. Unfair competition and free enterprise or some such . . .

(SHY *grabs her, sobbing and clutching her.*)

MISS MONA. (*Continued.*) Come on now, hunny, you're gonna mess up my outfit.

(*But* SHY's *like a puppy that's been saved from the pound.* MISS MONA *is somewhat moved by it, too.*)

MISS MONA. (*Continued.*) Oh Lord, girl, you got me on the edge of cryin'. And I've done retired from it. (MISS MONA *begins singing.*)

"GIRL, YOU'RE A WOMAN"

GIRL . . .
GET A HOLD NOW
STRAIGHTEN UP . . .
LOOK ALIVE . . .
GIRL . . .
YOU'RE A WOMAN . . .
YOU'LL SURVIVE . . .
REMEMBER
ONE GOOD THING WHEN YOU ARE MOVIN' ON
IS WONDERIN' WHAT YOU'LL FIND . . .
AND ONE GOOD THING ABOUT A PAST THAT'S GONE
IS LEAVIN' IT BEHIND . . .
GIRL, YOU'RE A WOMAN
KEEP YOUR HEAD UP HIGH.
GIRL . . .
YOU'RE A WOMAN
LOOK 'EM IN THE EYE
GIRL, YOU'RE A WOMAN
STARTIN' ON YOUR WAY
GIRL, I THINK THIS IS YOUR LUCKY DAY.

GIRL,
PULL IT IN NOW . . .
STAND UP TALL . . .
LOOK REAL PROUD . . .
GIRL . . .
NO MORE CRYIN' . . .
NOT OUT LOUD . . .
REMEMBER
ONE GOOD THING ABOUT THE TEARS YOU SHED
OH, YOU WON'T DO THAT NO MORE . . .
AND ONE GOOD THING ABOUT A DREAM THAT'S
DEAD
YOU'RE WISER THAN BEFORE
GIRL . . .

YOU'RE A WOMAN
KEEP YOUR HEAD UP HIGH
GIRL, YOU'RE A WOMAN
LOOK 'EM IN THE EYE
GIRL, YOU'RE A WOMAN
STARTIN' ON YOUR WAY
GIRL, I THINK THIS IS YOUR LUCKY DAY

(JEWEL *appears and takes* SHY *on a trip upstairs, going from one room to another, as the* GIRLS *transform her, somewhat, from the hayseed that* SHE *is.*

SHE *steps in* DAWN's *room and gets a beautiful long dress put on her.*

SHE *crosses, stumbling in the tight skirt, to* GINGER's *room and gets her hair transformed.*

SHE *sees a mirror, transfixed by her own new-found beauty and descends the stairs like a princess, except for her too large cowboy boots.*

SHE *freezes on the stairs as the bell rings.*)

GIRLS.
ALL SHE NEEDS IS A LITTLE BIT
OF FIXIN' UP
TO PULL HERSELF TOGETHER
SHE'D BE PRETTY IF SHE'D ONLY TRY
TO PULL HERSELF TOGETHER
AND I'LL HELP HER IT'S AS EASY
AS CAN BE
PRETTY SOON SHE'S GONNA LOOK
A LOT LIKE ME

MISS MONA.	GIRLS.
YOU'RE A WOMAN	ALL SHE NEEDS IS A
KEEP YOUR HEAD UP HIGH	LITTLE BIT OF FIXIN' UP
GIRL YOU'RE A WOMAN	TO PULL HERSELF
LOOK 'EM IN THE	TOGETHER
EYE	SHE'D BE PRETTY IF SHE'D
GIRL, YOU'RE A WOMAN	ONLY TRY
STARTIN' ON YOUR	TO PULL HERSELF
WAY	TOGETHER
GIRL, I THINK THIS IS	AND I'LL HELP HER IT'S
YOUR LUCKY DAY	AS EASY
	AS CAN BE

MISS MONA. (*Continued.*)
GIRL, I THINK THIS IS YOUR LUCKY . . .
JEWEL. (*Ringing bell.*) Company, Girls! Company!

(*A scared* YOUNG COWBOY *has entered and hovers near the door,
obviously afraid to take the next step.*

SHY *runs to get out of the way. The* GIRLS *all hustle into the
parlor taking up provocative poses, displaying their wares.*

MISS MONA *crosses to the* YOUNG MAN.)

MISS MONA. Howdy, son. Come right on in.

(HE *hesitates.*)

MISS MONA. (*Continued.*) They won't bite you.

(*The* YOUNG COWBOY *enters the parlor and moves through the
lineup.* EACH GIRL *comes on to him. Various ad libs such
as—"Hidy, Cowboy," "Wanta go upstairs, Good Looking,"
"Umm, umm." Until* GINGER's *"Hi, Junior."*

HE *pauses, looks out at the audience a beat. Then turns his
gaze to* SHY, *who is scratching herself, not knowing all eyes
have turned to her.* SHE *looks up. Shocked. Suddenly* SHE
starts to run OFFSTAGE. JEWEL *grabs her, turns her around
and pushes her* CENTER STAGE *to face the* YOUNG COWBOY)

SHY. (*Holding out her hand.*) Howdy.

(HE *shakes her hand. An embarrassed beat.*)

SHY. (*Continued.*) No kissin' on the mouth, this ain't the Junior Prom, you know.

(SHY *follows* JEWEL, *who heads for the bedroom.* HE *looks a little puzzled, but takes off after* SHY.

The music picks up again. And the GIRLS ALL *leave the stage
to* MISS MONA *alone.*)

MISS MONA AND GIRLS.
GIRL . . .
YOU'RE A WOMAN
KEEP YOUR HEAD UP HIGH
GIRL . . .

YOU'RE A WOMAN
LOOK 'EM IN THE EYE
GIRL . . .
  MISS MONA.
YOU'RE A WOMAN
STARTIN' ON YOUR WAY . . .

(*Music of song finishes without last line being sung.*)

BLACKOUT

ACT ONE

SCENE 4

An "ON THE AIR" *sign is lit, denoting a television studio. The* DOGETTES *begin to sing the introduction to* MELVIN P. THORPE'*s TV show.*

ANNOUNCER. (*Voice over.*) And now station K-T-E-X, that's, KTEX-TV is proud to present . . . that watchdog man himself . . . the eyes and ears of Texas . . . Melvin Pee Thorpe!

(*As* MELVIN P. THORPE *enters.* HE *is wearing a preposterous silver wig and a broad holier-than-thou smile.* HE *is a man of rapidly shifting moods—a preacher type with Show Business instincts masquerading as a newsman.* HE *holds his hands in the air acknowledging the* CROWD *cheers which are recorded. An* ASSISTANT *holds an* "APPLAUSE" *sign off camera and exhorts the* CROWD *to participate. The* MELVIN P. THORPE SINGERS *and the* DOGETTES *begin to drift Onstage during this opening monologue taking positions at microphones off camera and* THEY *react to the signs that the* ASSISTANT *holds up.*)

MELVIN. Arf arf arf. Rrww, rrww. Thank you, Texans. And welcome to "Watchdog," with yours truly, Meeelvin P. Thorpe, keeping an eye on what's goin' on in this beautiful State of ours. I have some very good news for you people. Last week's culprit has been brought to task! The makers of the Peanut Delight Candy Bar, caught in "Watchdog's Spotlight" have admitted that they put less peanuts in each bar than they advertise!

(*The* ASSISTANT *holds up a "*Boo*" sign. The* DOGETTES *"*Boo*".*)

MELVIN. (*Continued.*) But they have promised to mend their ways so from now on you can keep munchin' those Peanut Delights thanks to . . . WATCHDOG.

(*Sign held up reads in two parts "*Hoo*" and "*Ray*".*)

MELVIN. (*Continued.*) But don't forget to count your nuts!

(*Sign "*LAUGH — HA! HA!*" They* laugh.)

MELVIN. (*Continued.*) And now, neighbors, we have really come up with one this time. This week's Spotlight will shine on a situation that has been allowed to exist right in the shadows of the State Capitol! I'm talkin' about the Chicken Ranch, my friends . . .

DOGETTES. Oooow.

MELVIN. That's right and for those of you who don't know what is being sold out there in that innocent lookin' little town of Gilbert, presided over by that pseudo-righteous Sheriff, Ed Earl Dodd . . . I'll be as discreet as I can. A woman known only as Miss Mona is runnin' a house of ill repute.

DOGETTES.

OH NO!

MELVIN. That's about as mild as I can make it, friends. But why don't we just call it what it is? Let's get this thing out in the open. Isn't this the age of tellin' it like it is?

DOGETTES & MELVIN P. THORPE SINGERS. (*Spoken.*)
AMEN, AMEN!
HALLELUJAH

"TEXAS HAS A WHOREHOUSE IN IT"

MELVIN. Well, here goes and God forgive me. (*Spoken.*)
TEXAS HAS A WHOREHOUSE IN IT!
(MELVIN *claps his hand over his mouth.*)
DOGETTES/M. P. THORPE SINGERS.
LORD HAVE MERCY ON OUR SOULS!
MELVIN.
TEXAS HAS A WHOREHOUSE IN IT!
DOGETTES/M. P. THORPE SINGERS.
LORD HAVE MERCY ON OUR SOULS!
MELVIN.
I'LL EXPOSE THE FACTS

ALTHOUGH IT FILLS ME WITH DISGUST . . .
PLEASE EXCUSE THE FILTHY, DARK DETAILS
AND CARNAL LUST.
DOGETTES/M. P. THORPE SINGERS.
FILTHY, DARK DARK DETAILS AND CARNAL LUST!
MELVIN.
DANCIN' GOIN' ON INSIDE IT.
DON'T YOU SEE THEY'VE GONE PLUMB WILD
I INQUIRED, NO ONE DENIED IT.
NOW I THINK I'M GETTIN' RILED.

BODIES CLOSE TOGETHER
ARMS AND LEGS ALL RE-ARRANGED
AND THE SHERIFF DOES NOT CLOSE IT DOWN.
THAT'S VERY STRANGE!
DOGETTES/M. P. THORPE SINGERS.
DOES NOT CLOSE IT DOWN, THAT'S VERY STRANGE.
MELVIN.
MEAN EYED, JUICED-UP, BRILLIANTINED,
HONKY TONK COWBOYS.
DOGETTES/M. P. THORPE SINGERS.
OH, NO.
MELVIN.
MIXIN' WITH GREEN EYED, THIN LIPPED.
HARD AS NAILS PEROXIDE BLONDES.
DOGETTES/M. P. THORPE SINGERS.
OH, NO!
MELVIN.
NOT TO MENTION SOME TYPES,
THAT YOU'D NEVER GUESS WOULD VENTURE NEAR.
ACTIN' ALL DEPRAVED AND LOOSE AND WILD
NINETY MILES FROM HERE
(*Spoken.*)
HERE THEY ARE, OUR OWN MELVIN P. THORPE
SINGERS.
DOGETTES/M. P. THORPE SINGERS.
TEXAS HAS A WHOREHOUSE IN IT!
MELVIN.
I'LL NOT LET THIS SCANDAL FADE!
DOGETTES/M. P. THORPE SINGERS.
TEXAS HAS A WHOREHOUSE IN IT.
MELVIN.
I'LL UPROOT AND I'LL CRUSADE!

I CAN SMELL CORRUPTION AND I'LL FIGHT IT TO THE TOP!
 MELVIN/DOGETTES/M. P. THORPE SINGERS.
LOVELESS COPULATION GOIN' ON
 MELVIN.
AND IT MUST STOP! SSSHHH!

(*The lights go out.*)

 MELVIN. (*Continued.*)
AND NOW! HERE THEY ARE: MY OWN MELVIN P. THORPE
LONE STAR STRUTTERS

(*The* DOGETTES *do a flashlight dance as* THEY *sing the opening lyric.*)

 DOGETTES.
WATCHDOG WILL GET YOU
IF YOU DON'T WATCH OUT!
WATCHDOG SEES
AND WATCHDOG KNOWS
WATCHDOG KEEP US
ON OUR TOES!
WATCHDOG ASSURES YOU
THAT THE LAW'S THE LAW
NO EXCEPTIONS TO THE RULE
WATCHDOG AIN'T NO FOOL!

WATCHDOG PROTECTS YOU
HE'S OUT ON THE PROWL
GUARDS AND CHECKS THE BEST HE CAN
WATCHDOG IS A FIGHTING MAN!
WATCHDOG WILL THROW HIS
BEAM OF LIGHT AROUND
IF SOME FOLKS DON'T TOE THE LINE
WATCHDOG'S LIGHT WILL SHINE!

(*The lights restore and the* ENTIRE COMPANY *goes into a tambourine act.*)

 DOGETTES/M. P. THORPE SINGERS.
SHINE, SHINE, SHINE

SHINE, SHINE, SHINE
TEXAS HAS A WHOREHOUSE IN IT
LORD HAVE MERCY ON OUR SOULS
TEXAS HAS A WHOREHOUSE IN IT
LORD HAVE MERCY ON OUR SOULS
WATCHDOG SMELLS CORRUPTION AND HE'LL FIGHT
IT TO THE TOP
LOVELESS COPUATION GOIN' ON, GOIN' ON, GOIN'
ON, GOIN' ON, GOIN' ON, GOIN' ON . . .

MELVIN. Don't touch that dial, neighbors. I'll be back tomor-row — and the next day and the next — with new and revealing in-formation on this case. Watchdog never sleeps!

DOGETTES/M. P. THORPE SINGERS.
AND IT MUST STOP
WATCHDOG'S GONNA GET YOU
GONNA SHINE HIS LIGHT ON YOU
WATCHDOG'S GONNA GET YOU
GONNA SHINE HIS LIGHT ON YOU

ACT ONE

SCENE 5

Lights rise, a spot on a hallway in the interior of the Chicken Ranch. ANGEL *is on the phone.*

ANGEL. Hi, Mama! . . . (*Beat.*) I got me a job and I think it's gonna work out real nice . . . Uh-huh . . . It's a sales job. (*Beat.*) I don't know for sure, but I should be getting three days off in about . . . let me see . . . twenty days or somethin'. Can I talk to Little Billy? (*A beat.*) Mama, can we leave the Bible outta this? . . . I'll take him off your hands as soon as I get ahead a little. (*A beat.*) Please. Let me talk to Little Billy now, O.K.? (*Beat.*) Hi, hunny, how you doin'? Is Granny treatin' you good? (*Beat.*) Well, naw, hunny, I can't git there for Thanksgivin'. But I'll sure be thinkin' about you, tho'. Billy, now, don't go cryin' on me. You just gotta remember that cowboys don't cry! Have you made out your letter to Santa Claus yet? (*Beat.*) No! Well, you make it out and you get Granny to mail it to the North Pole, ya hear? 'Cause, Billy, I got a feelin' ol' Santa's gonna bring you a whole gunny sack full of play-pretties this year.

(*Beat.* Miss Mona *appears at the edge of the lighted area.* Angel *notices her presence.*)

Angel. (*Continued.*) Okay, hunny. I got to ring off now. Mommy loves you. 'Bye, 'bye.

(Angel *is near tears as* She *hangs up.* Miss Mona *comes to her now.*)

Miss Mona. We'll see if we can't work it so you get the curse around Christmas Eve, all right?

ACT ONE

Scene 6

Lights come up on Parlor. Dawn, *wearing an outrageous outfit, enters followed by* Beatrice.

Dawn. I just hope them Aggies don't win that ol' football game.
Beatrice. How come?
Dawn. Aw, they're always sayin' howdy and goin' Yee Haw. It just sounds so country.
Beatrice. Not near as country as you look in that Frederick's of Hollywood outfit.

(Shy *has entered,* Center, *wearing a 1950's ballgown and* Ginger *is fitting it for her.*

Linda Lou *rolls on in* Miss Mona's *wheelchair.*)

Linda Lou. (*Teasing.*) Hey, Shy, how was that ol' boy last night?
Shy. Aw, he was all right.

(*The* Other Girls *join in the teasing.*)

Dawn. Yeah, what kind of date did he want?
Beatrice. He looked to me like the eight dollar Tuesday night special type.

(*The* GIRLS *all laugh.*)

SHY. Naw, naw — He gave me fifteen dollars.
BEATRICE. Fifteen, huh?
LINDA LOU. Well, hello Mrs. Rockefeller!

(GIRLS *all laugh.* SHY *isn't sure how to take it.*)

GINGER. Ya'll just stop pickin' on her. I know how she feels. I still tell my Mama that I work in the Five and Dime.
LINDA LOU. Well, Hunny, you ain't lyin'.

(MONA *enters with* ANGEL)

MONA. All right now, Girls, you better get your behinds to work 'cause Jewel ain't gonna be here to help you all out.
LINDA LOU. I ain't movin'. The only rest I get around here is when I faint!
GIRLS. Awwww!
ANGEL. What's all the decorations for?
MISS MONA. The football players.
GINGER. Miss Mona, do we have to wear them ball gowns again?
MISS MONA. Yes you do and I don't want to hear any bitchin' about it this year either. Now you see hunny I try to create a homecoming dance kinda atmosphere.
ANGEL. It's gonna take me 20 minutes just to get in and out of the thing.
MISS MONA. Not these. Show her, Ginger.

(GINGER *grasps* SHY's *dress and tears it off with one swift jerk.*)

GINGER. Velcro!

(JEWEL *enters.*)

BEATRICE. Wow! Look at you!
LINDA LOU. Hey, Jewel, what're you sellin' today.
JEWEL. Hunny, I'm goin' to town with my man, and what I been watchin' you girls sell all week? Well, your Mama's gonna give it away tonight. And I'm gonna have one hell of a time doin' it, too. 'Cause when you only got twenty four hours off, you

gotta make every minute count. (SHE *punches a number on the jukebox, the* BAND *hits a wild sting, the lights flash like the inside of a jukebox and the number begins as* JEWEL *takes her place on the band stand.*)

"TWENTY-FOUR HOURS OF LOVIN"

JEWEL. (*Continued.*)
THERE'S AN HOUR OF HOLD ME TIGHT
THERE'S AN HOUR OF YEAH, THAT'S RIGHT
THERE'S AN HOUR OF BABY, BABY
COULD WE DO IT MAYBE
AGAIN.
THERE'S AN HOUR OF ME, OH MY
THERE'S AN HOUR OF LOW AND HIGH
THERE'S AN HOUR OF HONEY, SQUEEZE ME
'CAUSE YOU KNOW HOW YOU PLEASE ME
AND THEN
AND THEN, . . .

IT'S TWENTY-FOUR HOURS OF LOVIN'
TWENTY-FOUR HOURS OF FUN
TWENTY-FOUR HOURS AND HOW THE TIME DOES FLY
TWENTY-FOUR HOURS OF LOVIN'
LORD HOW THOSE MINUTES DO RUN
TWENTY-FOUR HOURS
HOW QUICKLY THEY GO BY.

THERE'S AN HOUR OF FINGER TIPS
THERE'S AN HOUR OF SWEET, SWEET LIPS
THERE'S AN HOUR OF A LITTLE LAYIN'
AND A LITTLE PLAYIN'
AROUND.

THERE'S AN HOUR OF THIS AND THAT
THERE'S AN HOUR OF TIT FOR TAT
THERE'S AN HOUR OF A LITTLE KIDDIN'
WHEN THE CHARMS I'VE HIDDEN
GET FOUND,
AND THEN, . . .

IT'S TWENTY-FOUR HOURS OF LOVIN'

TWENTY-FOUR HOURS OF FUN
TWENTY-FOUR HOURS AND HOW THAT TIME DOES
FLY
AND THEN IT'S TWENTY-FOUR HOURS OF LOVIN'
LORD, HOW THOSE MINUTES DO RUN
TWENTY-FOUR HOURS
HOW QUICKLY THEY GO BY
  (*Dance.*)
THERE'S AN HOUR OF PARADISE
THERE'S AN HOUR OF OOOO, THA'S NICE
THERE'S AN HOUR OF HONEY NEVER
HAVE I DONE THIS EVER
BEFORE.

'CAUSE THERE'S AN HOUR OF GETTIN' HOT
THERE'S AN HOUR OF THA'S THE SPOT
THERE'S AN HOUR OF I'M IN CLOVER
'CAUSE WE'RE STARTIN' OVER
ONCE MORE
AND THEN, . . .

IT'S TWENTY-FOUR HOURS OF LOVIN'
TWENTY-FOUR HOURS OF FUN
TWENTY-FOUR HOURS OF HOW THE TIME DOES FLY
TWENTY-FOUR HOURS OF LOVIN'
LORD, HOW THOSE MINUTES DO RUN
TWENTY-FOUR HOURS
HOW QUICKLY THEY GO BY.

(*As* JEWEL *finishes her number,* SHE *takes her overnight bag in
her hand, puts on her coat, and as* SHE *finishes the song* SHE
is gone.)

  GINGER. Well, I always wondered what she did on her day off!

(*Suddenly* SHERIFF ED EARL DODD *busts into the room.* HE *is a
big tall cowboy type, crusty, you might call him, complete
with six shooter and a star sherriff's badge.* HE *looks like*
HE*'s had a rough morning.*)

  SHERIFF. Goddamnit, Mona, I gotta talk to you! I'm so Goddamn mad my hair hurts. 'Scuse me, Ladies.

(*The* OTHER GIRLS ALL *respond.*)

MISS MONA. Alright, girls, why don't you run on up to your rooms and get ready to eat.

(*The* GIRLS *wander off into other parts of the house as* MISS MONA *goes to the* SHERIFF *to find out what in God's name is upsetting him.*)

SHERIFF. Did you see that God damn TV show last night?

MISS MONA. You know me, Ed Earl, I was home studin' my Sunday School lesson last night.

SHERIFF. Well, I was out in the cedar breaks all night myself lookin' for moonshiners, but I heard about it first thang this morning. It's all folks is talkin' about all over town.

MISS MONA. Well if they're talkin about television they're givin' me a rest.

SHERIFF. Naw, now! That's where you're wrong! That little television idiot that's always stirrin' up a stink? He told ever'body watchin' the news last night that you was runnin' a whorehouse, here in Gilbert.

MISS MONA. Did what?

SHERIFF. Hail, yes! Announced it right out loud! right on the goddamn news!

MISS MONA. Yeah, it was prob'ly news to a couple of tourists and all Texans still takin' their suppers outa high chairs. (*Beat. Then with interest.*) Did he call my name?

SHERIFF. Not only that, the sumbitch called mine!

(MISS MONA *laughs.*)

MISS MONA. He did?

SHERIFF. Now Godamit, Mona, you are takin' this thing too light. You forget what you're sellin' out here. But if that little television idiot goes on stirrin' folks up it's a liable to mess up your playhouse. Mine too, for that matter. I've stuck my neck out from Hell-to-Georgia protectin' you and there's some folks just might get to thinkin' it's because of them campaign contributions you give me.

MISS MONA. (*Teasing.*) Ed Earl, we both know that ain't even half the story.

SHERIFF. Me and you knows that, sure. And we also know that if you was not runnin' a clean place out here I'd close you down, faster than goose shit would run through a tin horn. But what about them forty-six hunnerd voters out there? A office-holder's gotta make ends meet just like ever'body else, and naturally he's gonna turn to his friends.

MISS MONA. Well, naturally.

SHERIFF. But the public don't unnerstand how politics works, no better than pigs unnerstands kissin'. Naw, Mona, if loose talk gets started you and me could both wind up with our tails in a crack.

MISS MONA. Aw, Ed Earl, would you come over here and sit down?

SHERIFF. Well hell yes!

(MONA *takes him by the hand and sits him down in her wheel-chair.*)

MISS MONA. You've got to learn how to relax. I know what you oughta do. Why don't you go unlock all that bootleg whiskey you've confiscated, see, and then you can call out the old church biddies in their fruit hats, and let 'em stand around clappin' and a 'singin' about Jesus, while you come in with a great big sledgehammer, and break it all up? It always worked before.

SHERIFF. Naw, you can't hardly git folks to come out to a whiskey-breakin' no more. Not if Lawrence Welk is on. Shit, I ain't caught me a peepin' tom in Lanvil County in twenty-two years, 'cause they're all at home watchin' the Goddamn television.

MISS MONA. Ed Earl, how are folks in town takin' all this?

SHERIFF. Well, okay up to now. They pointin' out how you always sponsor the Americanism pageant over to the high school.

MISS MONA. I hope somebody mentioned that I pay double taxes on this place as Miss Mona's Boarding House.

SHERIFF. Yeah but you let that television idiot keep on runnin' off at the mouth and folks'll start crusadin'. Preachers'll start gettin' everybody worked up, and the schoolteachers and the Jaycees, and I'll hafta spend so much time stompin' out grass fires I'd just as well to sell my huntin' dawgs.

MISS MONA. Ed Earl, don't you forget that one half of the police officers and two thirds of the lawyers in the state of Texas grew up right in this house. I think it'll all blow over in time.

SHERIFF. Goddamn goddamn television anyhow. Hell, their

ain't nothin' on it but meddlers and pryers and a buncha football boys jitterbuggin' in the end zones . . . You 'member, you 'member how nice and peaceful things used to be Mona? That was when you was still a workin' girl out here for Miss Wulla Jean. (HE *laughs*.) Why hell, back then when one a them little pissant nickel newspaper editors around here got it in his craw to crusade, I could always stop it by just threatenin' him. But goddamn, how in the hell am I gonna threaten Mike Wallace or Walter Cronkite? They'll be in this thing next.

MISS MONA. Aw, Hunny, now don't you worry . . .

(GINGER *runs* ONSTAGE, *interrupting the conversation*.)

GINGER. Sheriff! Sheriff! You better make tracks! The Mayor called. He's fit to be tied. There is a T.V. man down at the courthouse lookin' for you. (GINGER *exits*.)

SHERIFF. T.V. man? I'll betcha it's that Melvin P. Thorpe bastard. I better get on down to the courthouse steps.

MISS MONA. Well now, that must be some sorry reporter looking for you down at the courthouse.

SHERIFF. (HE *gives her a warning look*.) You know this Goddamn job ain't no fun no more? Hell, there was a time when law and order meant somethin'. But now, you gotta read folks their rights to 'em til you go half blind and fill out a stack of goddamn papers that a show dog couldn't jump over. I've got me half a mind to give this job back to 'em.

MISS MONA. Well, there's some say that you've got too rich for the job.

SHERIFF. Goddammit, Mona, that ain't funny. All I've got is my pension and my good name.

MISS MONA. And your cadillac and your cattle ranch . . . and how about that fishin' lodge down at Padre Island?

SHERIFF. Huh. Women'll drive you crazy if you'll let 'em. (*The* SHERIFF *exits out the ramp*.)

MISS MONA. Bye, bye Ed Earl. Y'all come back . . .

(*The spot holds on* MONA *briefly after his exit and we see her concern*.)

BLACKOUT

ACT ONE

SCENE 7

MELVIN P. THORPE *has deployed his* CAMERMAN *and his* SOUND RECORDER *into the street and* HE *begins to speak calling out to the* TOWNSPEOPLE.

"WATCH DOG THEME"

DOGETTES.
WATCHDOG ASSURES YOU
THAT THE LAW'S THE LAW
IF SOME FOLKS DON'T TOE THE LINE
WATCHDOG'S LIGHT WILL SHINE.

CAMERMAN. Cut.

MELVIN. Did we get it?

CAMERA MAN. Got it.

MELVIN. Good. We'll use that for the lead in. I wish you would of framed me against a better background. Is my hair OK?

ASSISTANT. (*With mirror.*) Looks great, Boss.

MELVIN. Okay, let's do it.

CAMERMAN . . . Rolling Melvin.

MELVIN. (*A monster smile.*) Howdy, good neighbors, this is the ol' Watchdog, Melvin P. Thrope, shining the spotlight on Gilbert — the little town with the big shame. We're on the courthouse steps to ask the local people how they feel about the infamous bordello running wide open in their American hometown. Good people! Good people of Gilbert! May I have your attention? I would like to speak about a matter of great concern!

C. J. To who, Me-e-e-e-lvin?

MELVIN. A matter of great importance to each and everyone of us.

RUFUS. Yeah, what's so all of a sudden important in this burg?

MELVIN. I believe that some of these church ladies over here will agree with me on this particular matter. Roll the playback.

K. C. Rolling.

C. J. Allright, let's hear it, Melvin.

RUFUS. Yeah, we can't wait.

MELVIN. Texas has a whorehouse in it!

DOGETTES.
LORD HAVE MERCY ON OUR SOULS!

MELVIN.
TEXAS HAS A WHOREHOUSE IN IT!
　DOGETTES.
LORD HAVE MERCY ON OUR SOULS!

MELVIN.	DOGETTES.
SIN IS RUNNIN' RAMPANT	OOOOH, OOOOOH
LIKE BEFORE THE FALL	AAAAH, AAAAAH
OF ROME	

　MELVIN.
SOMEONE IS PERMITTIN'
YOU KNOW WHAT . . .

(SHERIFF DODD *strides into the street.*)

　SHERIFF. All right, all right, let's move this stuff outa the way so we can get the traffic movin'. Out, folks, out . . . This here is a street, not a carnival. What are you doin' here . . . ?

(*The* CAMERAMAN *has moved around to get a better shot of the* SHERIFF. *The* SOUND RECORDER *has aimed his mike at him too.*)

　MELVIN. The only traffic in this town is what's headed for The Chicken Ranch, right, Sheriff?

(*A beat. The* SHERIFF *can't believe what* HE'*s heard.*)

　SHERIFF. Now, you got two tickets up to now! Paradin' without a license, and insultin' me. I said move it on out of here. Get off the street. (*To the* TOWNSPEOPLE.) Why don't you all go on home and watch some television?
　MELVIN. We're perfectly within the law here, Sheriff Dodd. As a newsman I've got First Amendment protection. The public has a right to know what's going on out there, and what kind of pay-off you're acceptin' to protect a notorious house of ill repute.

(*The* CROWD *lets out a moan, because* THEY *know what kind of trouble* MELVIN'*s in.*)

　SHERIFF. First thang. First thang is you're standing in Lanvil County, which by my figgerin' is about a hunnert miles west of that sinkhole you call Houston, an' I can't see it's a whole lot of business of yours what goes on here. (HE *wheels back on* THORPE, *his volume rising.*) Now, number two. Number two is, you ain't a officer of the law and I am, and this is my pea patch you're in. So don't go tryin' to tell me what my Goddamn job is or I'll take them dime store cap guns off of you and I'll whup your butt till it looks like peppermint candy.

(ONE *of the* CHOIR LADIES *has heard all of this kind of language* SHE *can take, and* SHE *departs quickly in shock. The* SHERIFF *once again starts for his office, but now* HE'S *about to explode, and* HE *spins around once again and the camera and sound are right with him. The* SHERIFF *is on the low side of screaming now.*)

SHERIFF. (*Continued.*) Now, number three, number three is, number three! No sawed off little shit is gonna accuse me of takin' a bribe and live to tell it, 'cause I wear the badge in this Goddamn County and if I get any madder I'm gonna blow your ass all the way back to Harris County and you can go see the Goddamn Civil Liberties Union in tiny little pieces. If I ever see any one of you sorry shitheads in this town again, I'm gonna lock up your ass until your baby's grown. If I even dream that any one of you bastards even thought about driving through here I'll hunt you down like a hound dawg would a coon. (HE *fires his pistol into the air and before the echo dies the street is empty.*) Gollamn wig-wearin' citified son-of-a-bitch. (*Beat.*)

BLACKOUT

ACT ONE

SCENE 8

The lights rise on the interior of the Texas Twinkle Cafe, a local gatherin' place for coffee sipping, beer drinking, barbecue eating and settling of the town's affairs, sexual or otherwise. It is Thanksgiving, the day of the Texas Aggie—Texas U. football game. DOATSY MAE, *a waitress who wasn't born yesterday, is behind the counter pouring coffee, filling sugar shakers, and generally preparing for the morning run.* EDSEL

MACKEY *is sitting at the counter.* HE *is the country editor of the local newspaper,* The Gilbert Gospel Mail, *and perhaps is the best educated man in town. There's a dry wit about him, and* HE *hides his keen intelligence behind country apparel and selected bad grammar. Probably many consider him the town Communist.* HE'*s a shrewd one, but* HE'*s learned in a small town that you have to trim back your sails and a bit of your spirit to get along.*

DOATSY MAE. (*Placing down beer.*) You want some pie with that?

EDSEL. Naw, that pie's been in that case so long it'd be like eatin' an ol' fren'.

DOATSY MAE. I hope you ain't gonna sit around playin' Will Rogers all mornin'. This ain't the day for it. You're gettin' nearly as handy with your mouth as the Sheriff is.

EDSEL. At least I ain't made no guest appearances on the "Watchdog" TV program.

DOATSY MAE. Can you believe they put him on TV, snortin' and acussin' and ashootin' that old thumb-buster of his? Run it right on TV.

EDSEL. I always said Ed Earl was the best argument I can think of for tough gun-control laws.

(TWO BUSINESSMEN *enter in a dither.* RUFUS POINDEXTER, *an automobile dealer who is also Mayor of the town, is dressed in a conventional suit and tie;* C. J. SCRUGGS, *insurance man and President of the Jaycees, is dressed in a super flashy sports coat, loud slacks, and louder tie.* HE *looks to be running for the Best Dressed Man Award and coming in last.* THEY *cross to a small table near the counter.*)

RUFUS. —which is shit for the birds.

DOATSY MAE. Mornin', boys.

RUFUS. Mornin, Doatsy Mae.

C. J. SCRUGGS. Hi, darlin'!

RUFUS. I've had calls from four preachers, six deacons, and the presidents of two garden clubs. Don't know why I let people talk me into serving as the mayor of this incorporated sandtrap anyway.

C. J. SCRUGGS. Well, my insurance customers called me all night long. Half of 'em insisting I sign that damn petition to close the Chicken Ranch, the other half threatenin' to cancel their policies if I do.

(THEY *sit at the table and exchange muted greetings with* EDSEL, *not anything effusive.* THEY *are the town's go-getters and leading lights, where* EDSEL *is more a thorn in their sides.*)

EDSEL. Mornin', Mr. Mayor.
RUFUS. (*Upset.*) Mornin'.
EDSEL. C. J.
C. J. SCRUGGS. (*With disdain.*) Edsel.
DOATSY MAE. (*Bringing them coffee automatically.*) Y'all wanna cripple that with a little dab uh cream?
C. J. SCRUGGS. Naw, I need mine as strong as bear hair this mornin'.
DOATSY MAE. Eggs or anything?
RUFUS. Naw, I'll do well to keep this down.

(DOATSY MAE *crosses back to her station behind the counter.*)

RUFUS. (*Continued.*) Damn Ed Earl Dodd for a pluperfect fool! That old fart'd screw up a two car funeral.
C. J. SCRUGGS. Well, I'd hate to see him be made the fall guy, when the whole town's knowed about Mona's place since Christopher Columbus.
RUFUS. Aw, C. J., his time's past. He can't run around here in the 1970's actin' like Matt Dillon with a toothache!
C. J. SCRUGGS. Maybe the Sheriff ain't the only one livin' in the past, Rufus. The Chicken Ranch served a purpose once. Aww, but everythang's opened up today. Why we've underwent a world wide sexual revolution.
DOATSY MAE. Well, it ain't reached 909 East Watermelon Drive.
RUFUS. How do y'all read the public's pulse about all this?
EDSEL. Oh, about fifty percent outraged and fifty percent self-righteous.
RUFUS. Well, I'd like to offer a little civic leadership. But I'm not damn fool enough to do it until I know which way the people want to be led.

(*The* SHERIFF *enters.*)

SHERIFF. Mornin' fellers.

(*The* BUSINESSMEN *turn away from him.*)

DOATSY MAE. Well, if it ain't the celebrated cussin' Sheriff of Lanvil County.

SHERIFF. Now, if you gonna be a all-mornin' smart-alec, I'll take my dime to the Cattle Call Inn.

DOATSY MAE. Why, Sheriff, when did they start makin' you pay?

SHERIFF. I ain't foolin', Doatsy Mae. You know, your jokes is just as bad as your coffee. Now give me a cup of the goddamn stuff.

(SHE *serves him and there is a long beat.*)

SHERIFF. (*Continued.*) Well, goddamn it, fellers, I didn't know that little shitass had them machines a-runnin'.

C. J. SCRUGGS. Well, you sure fixed our wagon, Ed Earl Dodd. All we wanted was to keep it quiet about the Chicken Ranch. Now it's the hottest thing on the air since the Gong Show.

EDSEL. And Austin's gonna carry it again on the six o'clock news.

RUFUS. Oh, my God! Ed Earl, ya can set up speed traps to catch the tourists, you can look the other way when the wrong kid swipes a car to go joy-ridin', hell, you can even allow Mona to run her place out there. But the one thing you can't get away with, Ed Earl, is broadcastin' gutter talk on TV!

SHERIFF. I didn't know he was takin' pitchers.

DOATSY MAE. What did you figger the camera was for?

SHERIFF. I'm gettin' just a little bit sick of all this bad-mouthin'! Hell, the Chicken Ranch don't give me near as much trouble as the roller-skatin' rink, or them all-night stag parties out at Legionnaires Hall. (SHERIFF *points to* C. J. *as the culprit and* C. J. *rises to protest.*)

C. J. SCRUGGS. Now c'mon, Sheriff, dang it!

(THEY ALL *get a good laugh at* C. J.'*s expense.*)

RUFUS. You oughta make that speech on TV.

C. J. SCRUGGS. The Jesus Bunch claims she runs off industry that might locate here.

SHERIFF. Horsecrap! She's the biggest industry in this county herownself!

EDSEL. And the Chicken Ranch don't even pollute the air or the water.

SHERIFF. If you was to show a little guts of your own, Edsel, you would stand up for your town in your newspaper, 'stead of runnin' all that sissy crap about glee clubs winnin' ribbons and old ladies holdin' ice cream socials in their back yards. That sawed-off little fart didn't let out no big secrets, you know.

(*The* BUSINESSMEN *say nothing.*)

SHERIFF. (*Continued.*) You guys have just all went apeshit. Hell, Miss Mona herself ain't all that worried about it. I was out there this mornin' and they was gettin' fixed up for the Thanksgivin' party, just like always.

RUFUS. (*Suddenly ruffled.*) Ed Earl, if that television crusader gets wind of those football boys bein' out there, I'm gonna move to Bankok.

SHERIFF. Well, I tell you boys this much: if that little three-foot excuse for a man comes round here again, I'm gonna flatten him so he has to roll down his socks to shit. (*The* SHERIFF *laughs uproariously at his own joke.* HE *pounds* C. J. *and* RUFUS *on the back and limps around the room in hysterics. Finally* HE *see* DOATSY *staring at him in disgust.* HE *sobers, gets his hat.*) Well, I guess, I guess I better get myself on back to my office so's that everybody can call me up and tell me we've got a whorehouse operatin' here . . . for about a hunerd and fifty years! (*The* SHERIFF *exits.*)

EDSEL. I'm not at all persuaded that I'd like to be standin' in Miss Mona's shoes right now.

DOATSY MAE. At least she ain't on her feet all day. I'd trade places with her.

EDSEL. (*Picking up newspaper and laughing.*) Somehow, Doatsy Mae, I don't think I'll hold my breath till you do.

(*The* THREE MEN *freeze in the background as a spot isolates* DOATSY MAE *and* SHE *sings:*)

"DOATSY MAE"

DOATSY MAE.
FREDERICK OF HOLLYWOOD'S

GOT THESE CLOTHES
IN A MOVIE MAGAZINE
YOU SEND YOUR MONEY
YOU TAKE YOUR PICK
YOU END UP LIKE A PLAYBOY QUEEN

I WANTED TO
I WANTED TO
BUT I NEVER COULD

WENT TO A COUNTY FAIR
SAW ME A SHOW
THEY HAD A GIRL UP THERE
SHE WORE A DIAMOND STUCK IN HER BELLY
SHE DANCED AND THREW AROUND HER HAIR

I WANTED TO
I WANTED TO
BUT I NEVER COULD

DOATSY MAE
PLAIN AS GREY
RESPECTABLE
DOATSY MAE
DAY BY DAY
RESPECTABLE
DOATSY MAE
THE ONE NOBODY THINKS OF HAVIN' DREAMS
AIN'T AS SIMPLE AS SHE SEEMS

SOME GIRLS HAVE CRAZY
SECRET THOUGHTS
THAT CAN REALLY MAKE 'EM FLY

SOME GIRLS CAN EVEN
DO THE THINGS
THEY MAYBE THINK THEY'D LIKE TO TRY

I WANTED TO
I WANTED TO
BUT I NEVER COULD

GOT ME A GARTER BELT
GOT ME A BEDROOM
SOMETIMES I CLOSE ME IN
DANCE TO THE MIRROR
THEN I CAN IMAGINE
I'M SOMEONE THAT I'VE NEVER BEEN

I WANTED TO
I WANTED TO
BUT I NEVER COULD

DOATSY MAE
PLAIN AS GREY
RESPECTABLE
DOATSY MAE
DAY BY DAY
RESPECTABLE
DOATSY MAE
THE ONE NOBODY THINKS OF HAVIN' DREAMS
AIN'T AS SIMPLE AS SHE SEEMS
DOATSY'S NOT AS SIMPLE AS SHE SEEMS

(*Lights return to normal.*)

DOATSY MAE. (*Continued.*) You boys want to see a menu? We got a nice hot turkey sandwich for our Thanksgivin' Special.

RUFUS. Naw, I got to get on home and see what kinda holiday surprise Doreen cooked up.

C. J. SCRUGGS. Well, I got to get ready to watch that football game. It's on TV at two. Them Aggies are gonna do some stompin' today. YeeHaw!

RUFUS. Five dollars says the Longhorns take 'em.

C. J. SCRUGGS. You on. Why, we got our best team since '39. On our best day we could beat them Dallas Cowboys.

EDSEL. Can I get some of that?

C. J. SCRUGGS. All you want, Teasipper. (HE *collects the money.*) Here, Doatsy. You hold the stakes for good luck.

RUFUS. Who do you like, Doatsy Mae?

DOATSY MAE. I don't like neither one of 'em, to tell the truth. But I'll tell you who I'd put my money on.

C. J. SCRUGGS. Who's that?

DOATSY MAE. Mona. Cause no matter who wins that ol' football game, she's gonna come out ahead.

(*The* THREE MEN *all laugh with her.*)

BLACKOUT

ACT ONE

SCENE 9

The ANNOUNCER *(V.O. on tape) begins speaking during the Blackout.*

ANNOUNCER. (*V.O.*)—and this football game has been a real stem-winder, just as the experts thought it would . . . and now, as the gladiators collect themselves during this time out, let's spend a few special moments with a bunch of kids as American as the Fourth of July . . . and as refreshing as country rain . . .

(*The downbeat of the "*ANGELETTE NUMBER.*" A spotlight hits the floor Stage Right. We are waiting for an entrance. Then a Texas Aggie* ANGELETTE *shuffles on sideways.* SHE *is dressed in an outrageous version of a drill team outfit, obviously selling sex.* SHE *is accompanied by a life-sized doll on each side attired identically, all with a wide-eyed, vacant smile.* SHE *shuffles to the Left proscenium and is joined by another* GIRL *with dolls as* SHE *reverses direction and shuffles back Right. This continues until there are* SIX GIRLS *with dolls and* THEY *do a close order drill tap routine.*

The VOICE OVER *continues all the while.*)

ANNOUNCER. (*V.O.*) (*Continued.*) There they are, the fabled Texas Aggie Angelettes . . . as fine a bouquet of long-stemmed American Beauties as you'll find. Each of these lovely girls is a member in good standing of the . . . Fellowship of Christian Athletic Supporters. Each and every Angelette carries a full scholastic load . . . as well as pleasuring herself with extra-curricular activities. Fifty-three percent of these girls are enrolled in the School of Religion . . . Forty-four percent are Home Economics majors . . . and the remaining three percent is into Animal Husbandry . . . Each Angelette is accompanied on road trips by a chaperon known as her Road Mother . . . and each Road Mother is responsible for the moral conduct of his, or her, particular Angelette . . . Now, before we go back to play, let's switch down to the sideline and to The Golden Voice of the Sunshine Network, Chip Brewster.

(*A typical* SPORTSCASTER *charges out, full of enthusiasm, microphone in hand.*)

TV COLORMAN. Hi, there, sports fans. I'm going to be talking with Imogene Charlene Greene, one of those fabled Texas Aggie Angelettes. We're going to find out a little about the wonderful lives of these wonderful precision girls. Imogene Charlene, you girls have to undergo quite a rigid program of discipline.

IMOGENE. Oh yes this is very true. A Angelette must be a very dedicated type of person.

TV COLORMAN. Fine, wonderful Imogene Charlene and just what does that require?

IMOGENE. Very much . . . dedication.

TV COLORMAN. Fabulous, wonderful and great. Most of you girls are beauty queens, isn't that right?

IMOGENE. Oh yes this is very true. Why I myself have been Miss Cooking Oil Concentrate, Miss High Heel Pumps . . . Miss Vocational Educational Opportunity . . . Miss G.I. Benefits . . .

TV COLORMAN. That's just wonderful, Imogene Charlene.

IMOGENE. . . . Miss Medical Alcohol . . . Miss TV Dinner and Miss Mistaken Identity . . .

TV COLORMAN. I know that you girls have high ideals and look up to the people who embody the qualities you most admire. Could you tell us quickly your three all time Great American Heroes?

IMOGENE. (*Caught unaware.*) Oh, Jesus!

TV COLORMAN. That's one, now name two more . . . Back to you, Bob . . . Oh my God . . .

(*The* ANGELETTES *do another turn and bow.*

As the ANGELETTES *exit in the dark, we hear the voice of the* ANNOUNCER, *amidst the cheers and cries of the football crowd.*)

ANNOUNCER. (*V.O.*) (*On tape.*) Back to play. (*A beat.*) The Texas Aggies trail with only three seconds left. They've got the ball on the six yard line and they need a touchdown to win. (*A beat.*) Bubba Schrake, the Aggie quarterback, looks over the defense. (*A beat.*) Charlie Wilson splits right, out wide. (*A beat.*) Schrake takes the snap, spins, hands off to Gary Cartwright. Cartwright swings wide . . . He's got running room . . . He could go, and he's in there! He's in for a touchdown! And the Aggies win it!

(*The Texas Aggie* WAR HYMN *begins.*)

ANNOUNCER. (*V.O.*) (*Continued.*) Kyle Field is going absolutely wild! And The Texas Aggies win it 13 to 12!

(*The music swells up and then fades out under the top of the next scene.*)

ACT ONE

SCENE 10

SENATOR J. T. WINGWOAH, *dressed in the almost obligatory uniform of the small town Texas politician, Stetson, dark suit, boots, string tie and belt buckle with the State of Texas on it, appears, and standing on a stool, finally gets the* PLAYERS' *attention, somewhat.*

SENATOR WINGWOAH. Boys, I want to tell you, that was the greatest victory since General Eisenhower won!

AGGIE 1. YeeeeHaw! Didn't them Teasippers step in a deep pile of Aggie shit!

SENATOR WINGWOAH. Now, Boys, let's keep it down. Somebody might have a microphone in here. Ha! Ha!

AGGIE 2. Did you see me knock that sucker's teeth out? Shit, a dentist couldn't a did it any cleaner. Yee Haw!

SENATOR WINGWOAH. I swear I think you boys coulda whupped the Dallas Cowboys today. It makes me so proud to be an Aggie. Why, there's never been a better bunch of scrappers out there than you boys. It's enough to make me break down and cry like a baby I'm so proud of you.

AGGIE 3. (*Tossing him a beer.*) Aw, come on, Senator, have a Lone Star on us.

SENATOR WINGWOAH. Why, you boys know Senators don't drink! It ain't good for the Baptist vote! But I know you boys been holdin' back all season on your beer drinkin' and . . . ah . . . other unmentionables. Ha, ha, ha.

SCANDINAVIAN PLACE-KICKER. (*In Scandinavian.*) Shit! I thought you promised to take us to a whorehouse.

SENATOR WINGWOAH. What the hell is that Scandihoovian place-kicker talkin' about?

AGGIE 4. He says you says you was gonna take us to a whorehouse. (ALL *the* AGGIES *agree, loudly.*)

SENATOR WINGWOAH. I did and I will, but let's don't blow no bugles! I always keep my campaign promises.

ALL AGGIES.
YEEEEHAW!

SENATOR WINGWOAH. But the Chicken Ranch ain't just any old whorehouse. It's a fine institution and I'm proud to have it in my district and I don't give a fiddler's fuck what Melvin P. Thorpe says! All right boys. Now let me hear it, YeeeeeeHaw!

ALL AGGIES.
YEEEEHAW! · ·

(SENATOR WINGWOAH *exits.*)

"THE AGGIE SONG"

WE GONNA WHOMP
AND STOMP
AND WHOOP IT UP TONIGHT
THOSE LITTLE GALS WON'T NEVER EVER BE THE
SAME
(THEY GONNA LOVE IT WHEN WE)
WHOMP
AND STOMP
AND WHOOP IT UP ALL RIGHT
IT'S EVEN BETTER THAN A AGGIE FOOTBALL GAME
   SCANDINAVIAN PLACE-KICKER. (*In Scandinavian.*)
BETTER THAN A FOOTBALL GAME?
THE CHICKEN RANCH?
   ALL.
AND THEN WE'RE GONNA SHOW THEM ALL

A THING OR TWO
WE'RE GONNA DEMONSTRATE
JUST WHAT
A CHAMPION CAN DO
YEEHAW

WE'RE GONNA PLAY 'EM OUT AND LAY 'EM OUT
TONIGHT
THEY WON'T HAVE NEVER SEEN NOBODY QUITE LIKE
ME – HUH
WE'RE GONNA WHAM AND BAM AND THANK YOU
M'AM TONIGHT
I SWEAR I DON'T KNOW HOW THEY'LL STAND SUCH
ECSTASY – HUH
(RIGHT BETWEEN THE GOAL POSTS)

WE BEEN DEPRIVED SO LONG
BUT NOW WE'RE GETTIN' SOME . . .
I BET THE GIRLS ARE COUNTIN' UP
THE MINUTES TILL WE COME . . .
 Aggie 3.
THEY AIN'T THE ONLY ONES
 An Aggie (*Solo.*)
75 MILES UNTIL WE GET TO HEAVEN
75 MILES UNTIL OUR PLANS ARE LAID
75 MILES UNTIL WE GET TO THE CHICKEN RANCH
WHERE HISTORY
AND AGGIE BOYS
GETS MADE
 All.
WE GONNA WHOMP
AND STOMP
AND WHOOP IT UP TONIGHT
THOSE LITTLE GALS WON'T NEVER EVER BE THE
SAME
YEE HAW, YEE HAW, YEE HAW, YEE HAW

WE GONNA WHOMP
AND STOMP
AND WHOOP IT UP ALL RIGHT
IT'S EVEN BETTER THAN A AGGIE FOOTBALL GAME
POC, POC, POC . . .
UG, UGH, SHUG, HEE . . .

AND THEN WE'RE GONNA SHOW THEM ALL
A THING OR TWO
WE'RE GONNA DEMONSTRATE
JUST WHAT
A CHAMPION CAN DO
  2 AGGIES (*Duet.*)
22 MILES UNTIL WE GET TO HEAVEN
22 MILES UNTIL OUR PLANS ARE LAID
22 MILES UNTIL WE GET TO THE CHICKEN RANCH
WHERE HISTORY
AND AGGIE BOYS
GETS MADE

(*The* AGGIES *dance.*)

  ALL.
ONE MORE MILE UNTIL WE GET TO HEAVEN
ONE MORE MILE UNTIL OUR PLANS ARE LAID
ONE MORE MILE UNTIL WE GET TO THE CHICKEN
RANCH
WHERE HISTORY
AND AGGIE BOYS
GETS MADE

(*As the* AGGIES *stand at attention the music changes to a roman-
tic version of* "GIRL YOU'RE A WOMAN".)

ACT ONE

SCENE 11

The GIRLS *enter in their ballgowns looking somewhat ill at ease,
but trying to walk and look like we can imagine* MISS MONA
has drilled into them. THEY *have corsages,* SOME *carry Aggie
pennants, their hair is done up to match the 50's Homecoming Dance look.* THEY *curtsy to the* AGGIES. *The* AGGIES
whistle and yell as the GIRLS *surround them and the* BOYS
make a circle and THEY *move in opposite directions in a
cotillion until* MISS MONA *rings the bell and* THEY *all pair
off.*

Except for RUBY RAE, *who is left out.* SHE *turns around,
disappointed.*

RUBY RAE. Shit!

(GINGER, *also partnerless, has made her way through the* CROWD.)

GINGER. Do you wanna dance with me, I'll lead . . .

(THEY *dance together.* SENATOR WINGWOAH *enters.*)

SENATOR WINGWOAH. Howdy, M'am, I'm Senator Wingwoah of the 19th district and Aggie class of '49 . . . Mighty proud to meetcha.
MISS MONA. Hello, J. T. How's Mary Margaret and the kids?

(AGGIES *and* GIRLS ALL *laugh. During this scene the* COUPLES *move to the bedrooms one at a time.*)

SENATOR WINGWOAH. Fightin' Communism!
MISS MONA. I'm a dedicated Capitalist myself. You got the check, J. T.?
SENATOR WINGWOAH. (*Producing it from his hat.*) I got it right here. (HE *proudly hands it to her.*)
MISS MONA. I don't see no breakage fee on here, J. T.
SENATOR WINGWOAH. Why, thunderation, Miss Mona! These old Aggie boys is awright!
MISS MONA. Well, I guess it is the Aggies night to howl. But, you know J. T., the Sheriff's very nervous about all this television stuff. We are under the gun, so you have your boys walk easy, all right?
SENATOR WINGWOAH. (*Brightening.*) Did you see me on the six o'clock news last night? I come on right behind the part where the Sheriff was cussin'. I *denounced* this place. Said the very idea of it was simply intolerable. Said it's a shame and a disgrace and a stain on the memory of Sam Houston!
MISS MONA. I hope you didn't say it oughta be closed.
SENATOR WINGWOAH. (*Hurt.*) Oh Hell, Miss Mona, I ain't no damn *radical*! But you know how politics is.
MISS MONA. Fraid I do, J. T. Ginger, hunny, would you please show the distinguished Senator from our district to a room? I know he must be tired.
SENATOR WINGWOAH. Yessum.
GINGER. Why, Senator, I'd be honored. (SHE *curtsies, then* . . .) Come on, J. T.

(SHE *leads the* SENATOR *off to a bedroom, and* MONA *is left alone on the stage.* JEWEL *brings her wheelchair and a ledger book.* MONA *puts on her reading glasses, and sits and begins to go over her books.* JEWEL *exits as the* SHERIFF *comes quietly in behind* MONA.)

SHERIFF. Howdy . . .

MISS MONA. Hello, Ed Earl. How's tricks?

SHERIFF. That's just what I was fixin' to ask you.

MISS. MONA. (*Archly.*) The children are nestled all snug in their beds.

SHERIFF. No sign of that television idiot creepin' around anywhere?

MISS MONA. Haven't seen hide nor hair of him.

SHERIFF. Well I been out prowlin' the back roads and everthang seems quiet. But I don't know, I just get this feelin' that he's out there somewheres. Same Goddamn feelin' I got durin' the Hitler war, just before they hit us at the Battle of the Bulge.

MISS MONA. Well, now, if it'll help you relax any, I still got some of that snake bite medicine in my private stock.

SHERIFF. (*Sitting down.*) Naw, naw, naw, I've give plumb up on whiskey. Hell, that stuff'll make you fight your people.

MISS MONA. I remember a time when that didn't worry you much.

(*The* SHERIFF *laughs.*)

MISS MONA. (*Continued.*) Hey, Ed Earl, I remember one New Year's Eve you come rollin' out here before the sun went down. You had already been samplin' that Early Times bottle. By the time the midnight kissin' got started you didn't know if you were fish or fowl.

SHERIFF. Didn't much care, neither.

MISS MONA. It took Miss Wulla Jean and two of us girls to pull your boots off.

SHERIFF. Yeah, when I woke up, I felt so terrible I just knowed I'd had a mighty good time.

MISS MONA. And I remember hearing tell about a terrible fuss you stirred up at the Pecos Rodeo.

SHERIFF. Now don't go remindin' me of that. Hell, I been tryin' to forget that for fifteen years. (HE *laughs.*) Oh Lordy, Lordy, we've been some miles, ain't we, Mona? Hell, I recollect when you first come to work here for Miss Wulla Jean . . . That musta been, what, twenty years ago? Why, you wudn't no older than that youngun Shy you took on last week. When I seen you climb down off the Greyhound at the Texaco station, I figured you needed some lookin' after.

MONA. Ed Earl, you always did get sentimental after midnight. Come on back to the kitchen and I'll fix you some coffee.

SHERIFF. I hope it's better than that stuff Doatsey Mae makes.

ACT ONE

SCENE 12

The stage is left in half light for a brief moment. The COUPLES *are in the rooms in shadows.* SOME *half dressed. We see parts of bare bodies, arms, legs, backs. All this through venetian blinds.*

Then suddenly, outside, a flashlight flips on. The beam sweeps the audience and we know the WATCHDOG *has arrived.*

The flashlight motions to FOUR SHADOWY FIGURES *in overcoats and* THEY *scamper up next to him.* FIVE COMMANDOES *tiptoe into the silent house.* MELVIN *searches the dark with his light, then shines it on the upstairs rooms and starts them up the stairs.*

THEY *position themselves outside the rooms, and on cue* THEY *pop the flash cameras on the loving* COUPLES. *Screams and* EVERYONE *scrambles. The* PHOTOGRAPHERS *flee as* MELVIN *waves them out.*

AGGIES *and* GIRLS *run wildly about and off.* JEWEL *runs out and rings the bell.* MONA *and the* SHERIFF *run out of the kitchen as* MELVIN *is disappearing. The* SHERIFF *fires his pistol in the air.*

The last PHOTOGRAPHER *snaps* MONA's *picture and runs.*

The SHERIFF *runs Off after them firing in the air.*

MONA *runs after him, screaming "Ed Earl."*

Spotlight on the BANDLEADER *as the stage empties.*

BANDLEADER. (*Sings.*)
AND SO THEY'RE OFF 'N' RACIN' . . . RUNNIN' NOW
THE SHIT HAS HIT THE FAN
HE'S CAUGHT THE SHERIFF
DEAD TO RIGHTS
THAT MEDDLIN' WATCHDOG MAN
RIGHT NOW WE LEAVE THE
CHICKEN RANCH IN TERRIBLE CONDITION
BUT WE'LL BE BACK TO
TELL YOU MORE
RIGHT AFTER INTERMISSION

END OF ACT 1

INTERMISSION

ACT TWO

SCENE I

The lights comes up and we see repeated the last section of The Raid.

The bell rings, PEOPLE scream and run, and the lights immediately fade: leaving SENATOR WINGWOAH and GINGER in a spotlight in GINGER's bedroom, and EDSEL and the REPORTERS in a spotlight on the pit steps. The SENATOR has been literally caught with his pants down.

As the GROUP OF REPORTERS speak, SENATOR WINGWOAH will struggle to get his clothes back on, with GINGER's assistance.

EDSEL. You mean to say, Senator, that you have no independent recollection of how you got to the Chicken Ranch?

SENATOR WINGWOAH. That's God's own truth. 'Course, now, I got my suspicions. I mean who's the most dedicated anti-Communist in the State Legislature?

EDSEL. I suspect you're about to nominate yourself.

SENATOR WINGWOAH. It stands to reason they'd want to harm my good name!

REPORTER 1. But how were you coaxed into a whorehouse?

SENATOR WINGWOAH. I'm surprised you boys hadn't figgered that out for yourself. I was doped!

(*The* REPORTERS *react.*)

SENATOR WINGWOAH. (*Continued.*) Yessir, Communists are always dopin' our college kids. I was easy prey.

EDSEL. Senator, there used to be a Communist over in Waco. But he died in '68.

REPORTER 2. Presumably then, these Communist agents stripped you and planted you in a strange bed?

SENATOR WINGWOAH. All unbeknowing to myself, yessir! But just remember that church ain't over til they sing! Once this thing has been exposed, I'll be vindicated. (*He zips up his fly.*)

AIDE. Ladies and Gentlemen . . . His Excellency, the Governor of Texas.

(*The band plays a fanfare which continues through the Gov-ERNOR's entrance.*

The GOVERNOR *enters, beaming and waving.* HE *is followed by* SENATOR WINGWOAH. *The* GOVERNOR *acts as if* HE's *receiving the plaudits of multitudes, throws his arms over his head and gives the V for Victory sign. Then* HE *suddenly and viciously silences the band and the cheer with a gesture.*)

GOVERNOR. My friends I want to thank you for that warm and sincere Christian welcome.

AIDE. Gentlemen, you may ask your questions now.

REPORTER I. Governor, Sir, what do you think of the ex-plosive situation in the Middle East?

GOVERNOR. Well, I was sayin' at the weekly Prayer breakfast, just this mornin' in this historic capital, that it behooves both the Jews and the A-rabs to settle their differences in a Christian manner.

(*His* AIDES *and* ENTOURAGE *applaud wildly.*)

REPORTER 2. How do you account, Governor, for the current high unemployment rate in our state?

GOVERNOR. Ain't nothin' unusual about it. It's just the natural law of economics. Now the real cause of this unemployment thing is that . . . people are out of work!

(*Once again wild applauses from* AIDES.)

THORPE. Governor: Governor. Melvin P. Thorpe, Watch Dog News. What about the Chicken Ranch, Governor?

(*A moment of shocked silence, then.*)

"THE SIDESTEP"

GOVERNOR.
FELLOW TEXANS
I AM PROUDLY STANDING HERE TO HUMBLY SAY
I ASSURE YOU
AND I MEAN IT
NOW WHO SAYS I DON'T SPEAK OUT AS PLAIN AS DAY?

AND
FELLOW TEXANS
I'M FOR PROGRESS
AND THE FLAG, LONG MAY IT FLY
I'M A POOR BOY
COME TO GREATNESS
SO IT FOLLOWS THAT I CANNOT TELL A LIE

> EDSEL. What the hell did he say?
>
> REPORTER 1. Mairzy Doats and Doazy Doats.
>
> EDSEL. And little lambs ee dyzy.

(ALL *freeze except* GOVERNOR *who does a sneaky dance.*)

> GOVERNOR.

OOOOOOOOOOO! I LOVE TO DANCE THE LITTLE
SIDESTEP
NOW THEY SEE ME, NOW THEY DON'T
I'VE COME AND GONE . . .
AND OOOOOOOOOOO! I LOVE TO SWEEP AROUND A
WIDESTEP
CUT A LITTLE SWATH AND
LEAD THE LITTLE PEOPLE ON.

(*Back to action and the* REPORTERS *begin to press in on him.*)

> REPORTER 1. Governor! Governor! Why do certain big banks receive special treatment when the state deposits its money?
>
> GOVERNOR. Sound business practices!
>
> REPORTER 2. Why don't you do something about industrial pollution? Even the Houston Ship Channel caught on fire.
>
> GOVERNOR. But we put it out!
>
> REPORTER 3. Do you plan to take action against the Chicken Ranch?
>
> GOVERNOR.

NOW MY GOOD FRIENDS
IT BEHOOVES ME
TO BE SOLEMN AND DECLARE
I'M FOR GOODNESS
AND FOR PROFIT
AND FOR LIVING CLEAN
AND SAYING DAILY PRAYER
AND NOW MY GOOD FRIENDS
YOU CAN SLEEP NIGHTS

I'LL CONTINUE TO STAND TALL
YOU CAN TRUST ME
FOR I PROMISE
I SHALL KEEP A WATCHFUL EYE UPON YOU ALL
 REPORTER 3. This is all going over my head.
 REPORTER 1. You and Wilt Chamberlain.

(ALL *freeze except* GOVERNOR.)

 CHORUS.
OOOOOOOOOOO! I LOVE TO DANCE THE LITTLE
SIDESTEP
NOW THEY SEE ME, NOW THEY DON'T
I'VE COME AND GONE . . .
AND OOOOOOOOOOO! I LOVE TO SWEEP AROUND A
WIDESTEP
CUT A LITTLE SWATH AND
LEAD THE PEOPLE ON . . .

(*Back to action.*)

 THORPE. Governor! Governor! Melvin P. Thorpe. Watchdog
News!
 GOVERNOR. Yeah, I got that.
 THORPE. Governor, why has the Chicken Ranch operation
been so long ignored?
 GOVERNOR. Beg pardon?

(*The* REPORTERS *are pushing in closer and closer.*)

 REPORTER 2. Sir, is it true that organized crime may be in-
volved?
 GOVERNOR. There's some acoustic problems in here.
 REPORTER 3. Aren't you worried about possible payoffs and
bribes out there?
 THORPE. Governor, Governor! Melvin P. Thorpe, Watchdog
News!
 GOVERNOR. (*Under his breath.*) Son of a bitch!
 THORPE. Governor, what are you prepared to do about the
Chicken Ranch and Miss Mona?
 GOVERNOR.
NOW MISS MONA
I DON'T KNOW HER

THO' I'VE HEARD THE NAME, OH YES.
BUT OF COURSE I'VE
NO CLOSE CONTACT
SO WHAT SHE IS DOING, I CAN ONLY GUESS.
BUT NOW MISS MONA
SHE'S A BLEMISH
ON THE FACE OF THAT GOOD TOWN.
I AM TAKING, CERTAIN STEPS HERE
SOMEONE, SOMEWHERE'S GONNA HAVE TO CLOSE
HER DOWN!

(HE *dances Off before anyone can stop him.*)

THORPE. Arf, arf, arf-rrrr, rrrr.

DOGETTES & M. P. THORPE SINGERS.

MELVIN THORPE HAS DONE IT ONCE AGAIN
HE SHONE HIS LIGHT
AND NOW WE SEE
MELVIN THORPE HAS GONE THROUGH
THICK AND THIN
AND LED US ALL TO VICTORY.

DOGETTES & M. P. THORPE SINGERS.	REPORTERS, AIDE & SENATOR.
MELVIN THORPE HAS DONE IT ONCE AGAIN	OOOO, HE LOVES TO DANCE THE
HE'S SHONE HIS LIGHT AND NOW WE SEE	LITTLE SIDESTEP, NOW WE SEE HIM
MELVIN THORPE HAS GONE	NOW WE DON'T. HE'S COME AND GONE.
THROUGH THICK AND THIN	OOOO, HE LOVES TO SWEEP AROUND
AND LED US ALL TO VICTORY	A WIDESTEP. CUT A LITTLE SWATH
	AND LEAD THE PEOPLE ON
MELVIN THORPE HAS DONE IT ONCE AGAIN	OOOO, HE LOVES TO DANCE THE
HE SHONE HIS LIGHT AND NOW WE SEE.	LITTLE SIDESTEP. NOW WE SEE HIM
MELVIN THORPE HAS GONE	NOW WE DON'T, HE'S COME AND GONE.
THROUGH THICK AND THIN	OOOO, HE LOVES TO SWEEP AROUND

AND LED US ALL TO
VICTORY.

A WIDESTEP. CUT A
LITTLE SWATH AND
LEAD THE PEOPLE ON.

(A break in the music and the DOWNSTAGE *area is empty and the*
GOVERNOR *sneaks away from the* CROWD *to be alone and*
with the audience. HE *gleefully begins to do a softshoe.* HE
is celebrating his ability to sidestep every issue as the
CHORUS *sings behind him.)*

ALL.
OOOO, HE LOVES TO DANCE
THE SIDESTEP
NOW, WE SEE
HE'S COME AND GONE
OOOO, HE LOVES TO SWEEP
A WIDESTEP
LEAD, THE, PEOPLE ON.

OOOO, HE LOVES TO DANCE THE SIDESTEP
NOW WE SEE HE'S COME AND GONE
OOO, HE LOVES TO SWEEP A WIDESTEP
LEAD, THE, PEOPLE ON.

(GOVERNOR *continues dancing with music only.* GROUP *singing,*
GOVERNOR *dancing.)*

ALL. (*Continued.*)
OOO, HE LOVES TO DANCE THE LITTLE
SIDESTEP
NOW, THEY SEE HIM NOW THEY DON'T
HE'S COME AND GONE . . .
OOO, HE LOVES TO SWEEP AROUND A WIDESTEP
CUT A LITTLE SWATH AND LEAD THE PEOPLE ON.

MELVIN THORPE HAS
DONE IT ONCE
AGAIN
HE SHONE HIS LIGHT
AND NOW HE SEE . . .
MELVIN THORPE HAS
GONE THROUGH THICK

OOO, HE LOVE TO
DANCE THE LITTLE
SIDESTEP, NOW WE SEE
HIM NOW WE
DON'T HE'S COME AND
GONE . . .
OOO, HE LOVES TO

AND THIN
AND LED US ALL TO
VICTORY.
HAS DONE IT ONCE
AGAIN AND LED US ALL
TO VICTORY

SWEEP AROUND
A WIDESTEP, CUT A
LITTLE SWATH
AND LEAD THE PEOPLE
ON.
HE LOVES TO DANCE THE
LITTLE SIDESTEP
AND LEAD THE PEOPLE
ON.

(*End of song — the* GOVERNOR *exits.*)

ALL.
OOO, HE LOVES TO DANCE THE LITTLE SIDESTEP
NOW WE SEE HIM, NOW WE DON'T
HE'S COME AND GONE

MELVIN. Three cheers and a gold star to our Governor who has agreed to do his duty by calling on local officials to "Kill their own snakes." . . . so once again, the Watchdog News bites as well as barks. Arf, Arf . . . (*Chanting.*)
"WE'RE A GONNA CLOSE MISS MONA."

(*The* GROUP *begins to march in a snakelike line around the stage wrapping themselves in Texas flags.*)

ALL.
We're a gonna close Miss Mona
We're a gonna close Miss Mona
We're a gonna close Miss Mona

ALL.
SHAME, SHAME, SHAME
YOU'RE RUINING OUR
GOOD NAME
SHAME, SHAME, SHAME
YOU'RE RUINING OUR
GOOD NAME

EDSEL. Have you gone crazy Melvin? What do you get out of jumpin' on a bunch of poor, social misfits, tryin' to scratch out a livin' sellin' cheap nookie in Gilbert?

MELVIN. The law is the law!

EDSEL. Melvin, within two blocks of this capitol building you can get anything done to you for money that you can get in Tangiers! Tongue baths, naked massages, midget fags, somebody ticklin' your ass with a feather.

MELVIN. If you know that for a fact, Mr. Newspaper Editor, it's your duty to expose it.

EDSEL. Melvin, I don't give a damn if folks occasionally want their asses tickled with feathers. I'd kinda like to think that's what heaven is all about.

ALL.

We're a gonna close Miss Mona	Shame, Shame, Shame
	YOU'RE RUINING OUR
We're a gonna close Miss Mona	GOOD NAME
	SHAME, SHAME, SHAME
We're gonna close Miss Mona	YOU'RE RUINING OUR
	GOOD NAME

(MELVIN *joines the* MARCHERS *as* THEY *leave the stage chanting.*)

ACT TWO

SCENE 2

The bedroom lights brighten to reveal ANGEL *and* LINDA LOU. *We can still hear chants in the distance. The* MARCHERS *have appeared in the audience, now carrying powerful flashlights which* THEY *shine on the stage and at each other as* THEY *shout at the house.*

As the insults are shouted, the GIRLS *become aware and begin to move out of their rooms toward the front porch, gathering there to see what is taking place in the darkened exterior.*

HECKLER #1 *runs toward the stage down* LEFT *aisle and hurls something at the whorehouse.*

HECKLER #1. Get out of our town! (HE *runs back to the safety of the* MOB. HECKLER #2 *runs down the* RIGHT *aisle and throws another object at the stage.*)

HECKLER #2. Go on back to Dallas! (HECKLER #3 *and* HECKLER #4 *appear in different aisles at a safe distance.*)

HECKLER #3. We don't want you in Gilbert!

HECKLER #4. Pluck the Chicken Ranch!

(MELVIN *begins to parade around the aisle strutting his stuff.* WINGWOAH *appears in the* RIGHT *aisle.*

The GIRLS *have begun to appear from various parts of the house, listening to the insults from outside.* MELVIN *begins to lead the chant "SHAME SHAME SHAME, YOU'RE RUINING OUR GOOD NAME".*)

WINGWOAH. Father, forgive them, for they know not what they do!

ANGEL. What kinda lash up we got out there?

LINDA LOU. Sounds like a vigilante group or somethin'.

(GINGER *crosses and goes out on the ramp. The* MOB *has retreated to safe distance.* WINGWOAH *is still in view, aisle* RIGHT. *The* GIRLS *drift out with* GINGER.)

GINGER. Look at that freak show! Ever nut in Texas must be out there!

WINGWOAH. Evil and corruption, get out of my district!

DAWN. (*Pointing.*) Hey Ginger, isn't that your friend Senator Wingwoah, out there?

GINGER. Where?

DAWN. Right over there.

GINGER. (*Waving.*) Aw, hi there Senator! How's your Tallywacker hangin'?

(WINGWOAH *runs to safety.* ALL *the* GIRLS *tease him, laughing at his retreat.*)

RUBY RAE. Come on back, Senator. We won't bite you!

ANGEL. Not unless you pay extra!

(THEY ALL *laugh.*)

SHY. Hey, there's that meddlin' T.V. man!

LINDA LOU. Hey Melvin, do you need a good bitch for your Watchdog T.V. show?

(MONA *comes out onto the ramp.*)

MISS MONA. What's goin' on out here?

(*The* MOB *is at a distance but we hear some shouts.*)

HECKLER #3. Get that filthy operation out of our town!

HECKLER #5. Dirty white trash pigs!

MISS MONA. Now where'd this all American circus come from, anyhow?

(JEWEL *comes racing out with a shotgun and hands it to* MONA.)

MISS MONA. (*Continued.*) Give me that thing, Jewel.
JEWEL. Yes m'am. You do it.

(MONA *fires a shot in the air. Screams from the* CROWD *as* THEY *run hysterically in all directions.* MONA *hands the shotgun back to* ONE *of the* GIRLS.)

RUBY RAE. That was a mean lookin' bunch, Miss Mona.
GINGER. Yeah, that Thorpe's tryin' to convince ever' body that pure good and pure evil is about to rassle to a dog fall.
MISS MONA. Well, it looks to me like the confused against the mistaken, with the well meanin' comin' in to screw it up on both sides.
GINGER. You reckon the Governor was just makin' political big talk? He ain't hit a lick since he announced he was closin' us.
LINDA LOU. Yeah, that ol' bastard, he don't keep one promise in ten.
MISS MONA. Yeah, but he's as unpredictable as a high wind and he'd probably score in the high 90's on a crazy test. Naw girls, I think we better keep out of sight. You run on up to your rooms . . . It don't look to me like we're gonna have any Guests come callin' with that mob out there.

(THEY ALL *go off to different parts of the house where we see them going about their business.*)

JEWEL. Yeah, even the Co-cola man says his wife won't let him make no more deliveries out here.
DAWN. (*Exiting to her room.*) Oh no!

(*By this time* ALL *of the* GIRLS *have exited to their rooms.* MONA *and* JEWEL *are alone on the lower stage.*)

JEWEL. We're in trouble this time, ain't we Miss Mona?
MISS MONA. It ain't what I'd call the ideal situation. How many of them politicians you reckon got elected by whippin' up on us?
JEWEL. I can count three in my time.
MISS MONA. Yeah, but you know ol' Miss Wulla Jean'd be back ringing that bell soon as the polls closed. But this is different what with television broadcastin' it from hell to breakfast.
JEWEL. I sure been disappointed in that old Sheriff.
MISS MONA. He's had his moments, Jewel. When I first seen

Ed Earl he looked like he had walked right out of a cowboy picture show. Tall and handsome. He had blonde hair then . . . Remember? I never told nobody this before, Jewel, but he took me down to Galveston for a night.

JEWEL. Is that right?

MISS MONA. It was Kennedy's inauguration and we watched it on television in a hotel room. That was high cotton for me, fresh out of the panhandle. I'd never seen salt water. I remember the sun was shinin' and the water out in the Gulf was so blue it ached my eyes. The sun was shinin' on Kennedy, too, but it must have been some kind of cold up there because Kennedy's breath made little clouds of smoke when it hit the cold air. That's how I remember that day. We had a champagne brunch and I ordered Eggs Benedict, which I thought sounded mighty high-toned. I didn't even realize the chef had messed up the hollandaise sauce. (*A beat.*) When he brought me back here, he pulled a gown out of a bag and kinda poked it at me like it might bite him, and said, "Here, Cakes. This here's for you." He never was worth a damn at grammar. But I never felt more like . . . Cinderella. Oh, maybe it was no more than a bread and butter note. But I remember the sun and that blue, blue water and President Kennedy's breath makin' little clouds of smoke. (*Bringing herself out of the memory.*) And the worst fuckin' Eggs Benedict I ever put on my tongue!

(JEWEL *laughs.*)

MISS MONA. (*Continued.*) Naw, Jewel, Ed Earl's never played in the major leagues before and maybe he's not cut out for it. Not now, anyway. Not anymore.

JEWEL. I'm real sorry for the troubles you've been havin', Miss Mona.

MISS MONA. Jewel hunny, don't feel sorry for me. No, I started out poor and worked my way up to outcast. You just got to learn not to expect nothin' out of life.

"NO LIES"

WERE YOU FIXING TO SAY A LITTLE SOMETHING 'BOUT
HOW LIFE DON'T SEEM TOO FAIR?
DON'T EVEN START
DON'T EVEN START

WERE YOU LOOKING TO GET A LITTLE
DISAPPOINTED
TEARDROP GOING THERE?
DON'T MAKE ME LAUGH
PLEASE DON'T TOUCH MY HEART

WHO SAID LIFE WAS A ROLLER COASTER?
WHO SAID LIFE WAS SWEET SURPRISE?
WHO SAID LIFE WAS A CIRCUS POSTER?
NOT ME!
NOT ME!
SO, ASK ME NO QUESTIONS
GIVE ME NO ANSWERS
AND I'LL TELL YOU NO LIES

  JEWEL.
WERE YOU GETTING YOURSELF A LITTLE MOODY
'CAUSE
SOME FOLKS ARE DOWNRIGHT MEAN?
OH ME, OH MY, AIN'T THAT A SHAME?
WERE YOU STARTIN' TO MAKE A LITTLE SPEECH
ABOUT
THE TROUBLES THAT YOU'VE SEEN?
PLEASE SPARE ME THAT SAD SELF PITY GAME

WHO SAID LIFE WAS A BOWL OF BERRIES
WHO SAID LIFE WAS PEACH ICE CREAM?
WHO SAID LIFE WAS A BOX OF CHERRIES?
NOT ME!
NOT ME!
SO ASK ME NO QUESTIONS
GIVE ME NO ANSWERS
I'LL SELL YOU NO DREAMS

  MISS MONA AND JEWEL.
WERE YOU THINKING THAT YOU WERE GONNA
MAYBE HAVE
TO LEAVE THIS LOVELY TOWN?
BEGIN AGAIN
HIT ONE MORE SPOT
WERE YOU FEELING A LITTLE LIKE A BABY WHO
JUST GOT

ITSELF KNOCKED DOWN?
YOU SAY YOU WERE?
I SAY WELL SO WHAT?

(*The* GIRLS *have come out of their rooms and gathered on the balcony.*)

   GIRLS. (*Join in.*)
WHO SAID LIFE WAS A SONG FOR SINGIN'?
WHO SAID LIFE WAS SUCH A SNAP?
WHO SAID LIFE WAS A BELL FOR RINGIN'?

NOT ME!
NOT ME!

SO ASK ME NO QUESTIONS
GIVE ME NO ANSWERS
AND I'LL HAND YOU NO CRAP
   MISS MONA, JEWEL, AND GIRLS..
WHO SAID LIFE WAS A SONG FOR SINGIN'?
WHO SAID LIFE WAS SUCH A SNAP?
WHO SAID LIFE WAS A BELL FOR RINGIN'?
NOT ME!
NOT ME!
SO ASK ME NO QUESTIONS
GIVE ME NO ANSWERS
AND I'LL HAND YOU NO CRAP
AND I'LL SELL YOU NO DREAMS
AND I'LL TELL YOU NO LIES, NO LIES

BLACKOUT

ACT TWO

SCENE 3

Interior, SHERIFF's *office. It is a beat-up old place: a scarred desk and a few old chairs sitting around with a telephone on the desk, FBI "Wanted" posters on the walls, a police radio microphone, and a single file cabinet might suffice to suggest where we are. The* SHERIFF *is talking on the telephone as* DOATSY MAE *enters bearing a covered tray of food.*

SHERIFF. (*Into telephone.*) Yessum, yessum, you ain't the first one to tell me that. Awright. (HE *hangs up the 'phone.*) I've had so many goddamn phone calls, I can't even leave to eat.

DOATSY MAE. (*Placing tray on the desk.*) Well, here's your curb service breakfast. I'll probably retire on the tip.

(*The* SHERIFF *uncovers the tray and peers at it supiciously.*)

DOATSY MAE. (*Continued.*) It's the same as always, Sheriff. Two fried blind with beeswax and bullets on the side.

SHERIFF. Why can't you just call it eggs, honey and biscuits like everybody else? All that cafe lingo sounds like a Chinaman's jabber.

DOATSY MAE. (*Grinning.*) I hear folks is runnin' up and down the sidewalks with two sets of petitions. One to close the Chicken Ranch, and the other to declare it a National Historic Monument.

SHERIFF. I'd just admire if you didn't talk to me about them Goddamn petitions 'til after I ate.

(DOATSY MAE *sits on the edge of his desk. The* SHERIFF *looks up from eating.*)

SHERIFF. You waitin' to see if it's gonna make me sick?

DOATSY MAE. Naw, I tried it out on my dog first. Just thought I'd be neighborly and take your plate back.

SHERIFF. Neighborly my hind foot! You and everybody else in this Goddamn town's been snoopin' around like you'd been hired to write a book. I could use me a little Goddamn peace and quiet around here, 'cause I got me some hard thinking to do.

DOATSY MAE. Yeah you're under enough of a handicap as it is.

(*In come, rapidly and suddenly,* C. J. SCRUGGS, *and* MAYOR RUFUS POINDEXTER.)

C. J. SCRUGGS. (*Rapidly and without pleasantries.*) Dammit Sheriff, you can't hear nothin' except this Goddamn talk about the Chicken Ranch. Why it's like a broke record: CHICKEN

RANCH, CHICKEN RANCH, CHICKEN RANCH, CHICKEN RANCH. Now what the hell you gonna do about it?

SHERIFF. Scruggs, there's some folk just won't do to fart with and I'm one of 'em. Now you jes' leave the lawin' to me.

C. J. SCRUGGS. But nobody's buyin' nothin'. People just standin' around in clumps, wringing their hands and talkin' about this damned mess.

RUFUS. And I'm havin' to spend all my time playin' mayor. Hadn't sold a car all week.

DOATSY MAE. She ain't got a handful of supporters left, Ed Earl.

C. J. SCRUGGS. See there?

RUFUS. I gotta admit I don't care for the publicity. Not good for business. Not good for the town.

C. J. SCRUGGS. Course not. And you can't just sit around waiting to grow tits. You gotta do something. And now everybody's goin' ape shit over this Mafia scare.

DOATSY MAE. Yeah, they're afraid you'll start findin' bodies wearing cement overcoats.

SHERIFF. Doatsy Mae you just gonna have to clear on out of here now, 'cause we got some men talking to do.

DOATSY MAE. Yeah, I see what you mean. You fellas done such a good job on this thing so far. Keep up the good work. (SHE leaves.)

C. J. SCRUGGS. Now the Governer said he'd call out the Texas Rangers.

SHERIFF. He don't need no Goddamn Rangers! I got myself a purty good bullshit detector, boys, and I can damn sure tell when somebody's pissin' on my boots and tellin' me it's a rainstorm. The damn Governor is just trying to keep the television idiot happy and cozy up to the Jesus Bunch. If he's so all fired keen about closin' Miss Mona down, all in hell he's gotta do is give me one little bitty phone call and I'll do it. Hells fire, I wouldn't have no choice.

C. J. SCRUGGS. Well then why you got to wait for his phone call? Why can't you just take the bull by the horns an' take care of it yourself?

SHERIFF. Scruggs . . . I'm gettin' just a little bit sick of your Goddamn whinin' . . . Now you's willin' enuf to keep your eyes closed as long as we had a bird's nest on the ground, so I don't wanta hear . . .

(*The telephone rings.*)

SHERIFF. (*Continued.*) A man can't even digest his food. (HE *lifts the receiver.*) Uh, this is Sheriff Dodd speakin' . . . (*A few beats while* HE *is receiving the disturbing news.*) Awright, Governor. All ya had to do was ask. We'd a handled this thang locally if y'all hadn't let it get on Johnny Carson. (*A beat.*) Don't you worry about it none, Governor, you hold the whip hand, yes sir . . . yes sir . . . (*The* SHERIFF *hangs up the phone.* HE *suddenly looks old and broken.*) Goddamn if I don't feel like a country dawg in the city. If I stand still they'll fuck me, if I run they'll bite me in the ass. Well, I reckon you boys heard it.

C. J. SCRUGGS. You really gonna do it, Ed Earl? You gonna close 'er down?

SHERIFF. I said I would didn't I? There's some cats just can't be put back in the sack. (HE *rises, shifts his gun belt, and reaches for his hat.* THEY *file out.*)

"GOOD OLD GIRL"

WELL, SHE'S A GOOD OLD GIRL
WE'VE BEEN SOME LONG, LONG MILES TOGETHER
AND THANK THE LORD SHE NEVER WAS THE
CLINGIN' KIND.

BUT SHE'S A GOOD OLD GIRL
WE'VE HAD SOME FINE, BIG LAUGHS TOGETHER
AND I ADMIRED THE WAY SHE ALMOST READ MY
MIND.

NEVER TALKED NO FOOLISH TALK
HAD NO TIES AND HELD NO RULES
HELL, THAT GOOD OLD GIRL AND ME,
WE AIN'T, DAMN FOOLS YOU KNOW.

WE NEVER TALKED TOO MUCH
WE DIDN'T HOLD TO CONVERSATION
THERE'S LOTS OF THINGS I COULD HAVE TOLD HER
. . . I SUPPOSE
BUT WHAT I WOULD WANT TO TELL THAT GOOD OLD
GIRL,
SHE KNOWS.

(HE *crosses to the telephone and starts to lift the receiver.* HE

dials and MONA *comes to the telephone at the proscenium.
We see the conversation take place in mime. The* COWBOYS
*sing the chorus in the background, leaning on poles, steps,
whatever is available, as if* THEY *are lounging around the
storefronts in the town.*

MONA *mounts the steps, calls the* GIRLS *together and tells
them the bad news.* THEY *react in various degress of shock,
sadness, anger as* THEY *go back to their rooms and* MONA
turns DOWNSTAGE *as the* SHERIFF *crosses to leave, pauses,
sings the last line and crosses out.)*

COWBOYS.
WELL, SHE'S A GOOD OLD GIRL
WE'VE BEEN SOME LONG, LONG MILES TOGETHER
AND THANK THE LORD SHE NEVER WAS THE
CLINGIN' KIND

NEVER TALKED NO FOOLISH TALK
HAD NO TIES AND HELD NO RULES
NO, THAT GOOD OLD GIRL AND ME,
WE AIN'T DAMN FOOLS YOU KNOW

WE NEVER TALKED TOO MUCH
WE DIDN'T HOLD TO CONVERSATION
THERE'S LOTS OF THINGS I COULD HAVE
TOLD HER I SUPPOSE
  SHERIFF.
BUT WHAT I WOULD WANT TO TELL
THAT GOOD OLD GIRL
SHE KNOWS

(SHERIFF *exits.*)

ACT TWO

SCENE 4

ANGEL *comes* UPSTAGE CENTER *and sings the first section, then
goes to her room.*

"HARD CANDY CHRISTMAS"

ANGEL.
HEY, MAYBE I'LL DYE MY HAIR
MAYBE I'LL MOVE SOMEWHERE
MAY I'LL GET A CAR
MAYBE I'LL DRIVE SO FAR
THEY'LL ALL LOSE TRACK

(*The* GIRLS *are in their rooms, packing, making up, changing their clothes to leave the Chicken Ranch for the last time.* THEY *stop and sing their individual verses.*)

LINDA LOU.
ME, I'LL BOUNCE RIGHT BACK
GINGER.
MAYBE I'LL SLEEP REAL LATE
MAYBE I'LL LOSE SOME WEIGHT
MAYBE I'LL CLEAR MY JUNK
LINDA LOU.
MAYBE I'LL JUST GET DRUNK
ON APPLE WINE
ANGEL.
ME, I'LL BE JUST
FINE AND DANDY
LORD, IT'S LIKE A HARD CANDY CHRISTMAS
I'M BARELY GETTIN' THROUGH TOMORROW
STILL I CAN'T LET SORROW
BRING ME WAY DOWN
ANGEL, DAWN, LINDA LOU AND GINGER.
I'LL BE.
FINE AND DANDY
LORD IT'S LIKE A HARD CANDY CHRISTMAS
ANGEL, DAWN, GINGER, LINDA LOU.
I'M BARELY GETTIN' THROUGH TOMORROW
STILL I CAN'T LET SORROW
BRING ME WAY DOWN.
RUBY RAE.
HEY MAYBE I'LL LEARN TO SEW
MAYBE I'LL JUST LIE LOW
MAYBE I'LL HIT THE BARS

MAYBE I'LL COUNT THE STARS
UNTIL THE DAWN
  BEATRICE.
ME, I WILL GO ON
  GINGER.
MAYBE I'LL SETTLE DOWN
  LINDA LOU.
MAYBE I'LL JUST LEAVE TOWN
  BEATRICE.
MAYBE I'LL HAVE SOME FUN
  DAWN.
MAYBE I'LL MEET SOMEONE
AND MAKE HIM MINE
  ANGEL.
ME, I'LL BE JUST
  ALL GIRLS.
FINE AND DANDY
LORD, IT'S LIKE A HARD CANDY CHRISTMAS
I'M BARELY GETTIN' THROUGH TOMORROW
STILL I CAN'T LET SORROW
BRING ME WAY DOWN

  GINGER. Would you believe I'm gonna miss this rat hole?

  LINDA LOU. Well, you're crazy, too.

  GINGER. No, I just got in the habit of havin' a permanent address. It's the next best thing to a home I've had since the Okay Corral Trailer Park back in Wichita Falls. One night I was out honky tonkin' and when I come home my bastard husband had hitched up our trailer to a truck and hauled ass. Somebody said he went up to work on the Alaska Pipeline. (*A beat.*) Well didn't this whole Melvin Thorpe thing surprise you, Miss Linda Lou?

  LINDA LOU. Nothin' surprises me nowadays. If somebody told me it was snowin' shit, I'd just ask 'em if it was chicken or horse and how many inches.

  ANGEL. Oh God, when I first started hustlin' I thought sure I'd wind up one of them high priced city call girls. You know, silks and furs and sports cars and slinkin' around in soft lights geared to help my makeup work. I mean, why not? My face don't stop no clocks. So how'd I wind up on a four dollar mattress?

(SHY *appears from her room, carrying a suitcase and dressed for the road.* SHE *has the breezy air of a kid anticipating a new adventure.*)

SHY. It's about as cheerful in here as a funeral parlor.

GINGER. Well, Kid, I guess you just ain't been around long enough to grow any roots.

SHY. What difference does it make where we do what we do? I mean, it ain't like we gotta carry no heavy equipment around with us.

ANGEL. Shy, hunny, you're gonna do all right in this dirty business.

SHY. Well baby, it takes one to know one . . . Look, I know everything's a mess . . . and I care about it. I just can't help but feelin' like a little kid going on a trip!

GINGER. Maybe you ought to try Las Vegas.

LINDA LOU. Aw, get off it.

GINGER. Man, I made me a shit-pot full of money out there one time . . . Workin' them big hotels and casinos. All them conventioneers away from Mama and feelin' wild.

SHY. Well, why don't we go to Vegas and team up?

GINGER. Hunny, I've lost a step. Shreveport's more my speed right now. Just call me Sadie Motel. Open twenty-four hours. Hot and cold runnin' drunks. Waking up ever' mornin' to somebody else's bad breath. Somehow . . . it just never seemed to be quite like that around here.

ANGEL. Well . . . I'm going home to see my kid.

LINDA LOU. Come on, girl. You're gonna be screwin' for money as soon as you get your little bags unpacked.

ANGEL. Don't bet on it. This time I'm really gettin' out . . . This time I'm goin' home for Christmas, and I'm gettin' me a straight job, and I'm gonna like it!

LINDA LOU. Maybe so. But you'll never own a yacht.
ME, I'LL BE JUST
FINE AND DANDY
LORD IT'S LIKE A HARD CANDY CHRISTMAS
I'M BARELY GETTIN' THROUGH TOMORROW
STILL I CAN'T LET SORROW
BRING ME WAY DOWN,
I'LL BE FINE AND DANDY
LORD, IT'S LIKE A HARD CANDY CHRISTMAS
I'M BARELY GETTIN' THROUGH TOMORROW
STILL I CAN'T LET SORROW
BRING ME WAY DOWN

I'LL BE FINE AND DANDY

LORD, IT'S LIKE A HARD CANDY CHRISTMAS
I'M BARELY GETTIN' THROUGH TOMORROW
STILL I CAN'T LET SORROW
BRING ME WAY DOWN
I'LL BE FINE
I'LL BE FINE
I'LL BE FINE

(As the GIRLS *leave the Chicken Ranch carrying suitcases during the last strains of the song, the* SHERIFF *has appeared on the porch and* HE *tips his hat to them sadly as* THEY *leave.*

MONA *and* JEWEL *enter with their bags and the wheel-chair.* THEY *are dressed for traveling. This is the first time we've seen* MONA *dressed differently, in a western shirt, boots, western pants, and perhaps holding on to her fur.)*

ACT TWO

SCENE 5

As the last GIRL *leaves, the* SHERIFF *is left standing in the door-way.* HE *is awkwardly twisting and turning his cowboy hat in his hands.*

SHERIFF. Howdy, Jewel.

JEWEL. Sheriff. I'll be out in the car, Miss Mona. (JEWEL *leaves.*)

SHERIFF. (SHERIFF *stays near the door, uncomfortable with emotional moments.*) You awright, Mona?

MISS MONA. Hadn't felt so good since I had the measles.

SHERIFF. Well, just *Goddamn* ever'thing!

MISS MONA. Ed Earl, the best thing you can do is put this all behind you, just as quick as you can. (SHE *crosses around the wheelchair and sits in it* — CENTER)

SHERIFF. No, by God. Nosir! The damn little television idiot, and that goody-two-shoes governor, and all them folks that turned tail when this thang broke open? Some of 'em claimin' to be my frens, by God! Folks I've broke bread with and run rabbits with and took home when they was drunk! Well, I *owe* them damn people somethin', Mona, and I always pay my debts. (*A beat or two. The more* HE *thinks about it, the more it irritates him.*) I still just don't understand how this thang turned to clabber the way it done. I sure as hail don't. It just got outa hand. It ate me up before I knowed it was hungry!

MISS MONA. Ed Earl, I made a lotta money. I had a few laughs, I danced a bit. It's just time to pay the fiddler, that's all.

SHERIFF. Goddamn, Goddamn, if I just hand't cussed on goddamn television . . .

MISS MONA. It's *over*, Ed Earl! *Jesus*!

(*A beat.*)

SHERIFF. (HE*'s gettng uncomfortable.*) You likely to get right lonesome out there on that farm.

MISS MONA. Well, now maybe you come over to East Texas every now and again, and hunt squirrels . . . or something.

SHERIFF. Well . . . (*A beat.*) You or the girls need a ride or anything?

MISS MONA. Naw. I got my pick-up truck and Jewel's car. But you might see if you can keep those newspaper and television boys from houndin' us outta town. If you can do it short of killin'.

SHERIFF. Aw, now don't you worry about that none. Hell I got them peckerwoods roped off a mile each side of your gate. I got deputies and constables and highway patrolmen holdin' 'em back till hell won't have it.

MISS MONA. That's good, Ed Earl.

SHERIFF. Well, I guess I better get myself on back into town, and start stomping out grass fires. There's still lotsa folks stirred up, you know.

MISS MONA. I know. You go on.

(*A beat. The* SHERIFF *rises, then slowly goes out ramp.*)

MISS MONA. (*Continued.*) Ed Earl!

(*The* SHERIFF *stops and whirls to face her.*)

SHERIFF. Yeah, Mona?

MISS MONA. Do you remember President Kennedy's inauguration speech?

SHERIFF. Well now, here let me see now . . . uh . . . That's the one where he said ask your country not to do somethin' for you, you do somethin' for your country . . . ain't that the one?

MISS MONA. Somethin' like that. (*A beat.*) You remember where you were when you heard it?

SHERIFF. By God cakes, that's been, what? Must be twenny years ago. Ain't it? Why?

MISS MONA. No particular reason. I just seem to have that day on my mind, that's all.

SHERIFF. But I recollect where I was when Oswald shot him. Yeah, I'd just picked up three Meskin kids—they'd stole theirselves a goat from old man W. B. Starr and was throwin' theirselves a barbeque. (HE *laughs.*) Don't you see, I was jes' out on routine patrol, and I seen this smoke comin' up from old man Starr's pasture? Well, I parked my car in a ditch and I snuck up on them little greasers—they was barbercuin' that goat on a mesquite tree spitz, and sloshin' on the barbecue sauce enough for LBJ. That proved it was pre-med-i-tated, them havin' that sauce, don't you see? So we got 'em for Goddamn *felons.* Anyhow, I'd just slapped the cuffs on them little peckerwoods and marched 'em in lock-step back to the car when it come across the po-lice radio that ol' Kennedy had been shot up in Dallas. I 'member it all just as clear as a bell. (*A beat.*) It's funny, there's certain thangs you just can't hardly forget.

MISS MONA. A-men to that, Ed Earl.

SHERIFF. Now, when Jack Ruby shot ol' Oswald? Why hail, I asseled around and missed that! I damn sure did! Only live killin' they ever put on TV—hail, just about the only decent thang that was ever *on* TV in all history. And I asseled around and missed it. I damn sure did. A-course, I seen all them old films of it that they run over and over. They run 'em til they blame near wore it out. But it wasn't quite the same thang as seein' something without knowin' it was gonna happen.

MISS MONA. It never is, Ed Earl.

(*The musical introduction to "THE BUS FROM AMARILLO"*)

MISS MONA. (*Continued.*) I guess you better run along now.

SHERIFF. Well, right. Yeah, I gotta be runnin'. (HE *turns and slowly exits.*)

(MISS MONA *is left alone on the stage.* MONA *sings:*)

"THE BUS FROM AMARILLO"

MISS MONA.
CAUGHT A BUS IN AMARILLO

IT WAS GOIN' TO SAN ANTONE
HAD A BRAND NEW CARDBOARD SUITCASE
AND A WINDOW SEAT ALONE

AND I THOUGHT THAT I WAS SOMETHING
AND I DREAMED I'D TRAVEL FAR
MAYBE BE A RESTAURANT HOSTESS
MAYBE BE A MOVIE STAR

AND THE BUS FROM AMARILLO
RACED A TRAIN ALONG THE TRACK
AND I NEVER LOOKED BEHIND ME
'CAUSE I WASN'T COMIN' BACK

I HAD A ONE WAY TICKET TO NOWHERE
I WAS FINALLY TRAVELIN' FREE
I HAD A ONE WAY TICKET TO GO WHERE
ANYTHING WAS POSSIBLE FOR ME.

WE WERE DRIVIN' ON THROUGH CISCO
ON OUR WAY AROUND TO BAIRD
GOT A SUDDEN FUNNY FEELIN'
AND I KNEW THAT I WAS SCARED.

I WAS SHAKIN' LIKE A LEAF
AS WE WERE COMIN' 'ROUND THE CURVE
HAD THE SUITCASE, HAD THE TICKET
BUT I DIDN'T HAVE THE NERVE.

YES THE BUS FROM AMARILLO
HAD ME SO DAMN TERRIFIED
THAT I GOT OFF AT THE NEXT STOP
AND I NEVER TOOK THAT RIDE.

DIDN'T WANT THAT ONE WAY TICKET TO NOWHERE
DIDN'T WANT THE TRAVELIN' FREE
DIDN'T WANT THAT ONE WAY TICKET TO GO WHERE
ANYTHING WAS POSSIBLE FOR ME.

WELL IT'S HARD NOW TO DETERMINE
HOW A PLAN JUST DISAPPEARS
HOW THE DAYS CAN TURN TO WEEKS
AND HOW THE WEEKS CAN TURN TO YEARS

AND IT'S FUNNY HOW YOU WAIT FOR THINGS
AND WANT THAT LUCKY DAY
AND IT'S FUNNY, WHEN THE BUS STOPPED
I GOT OFF AND WALKED AWAY

AND THE BUS FROM AMARILLO
I CAN HEAR IT STILL GO BY
GUESS I MISSED MY ONLY CHANCE
AND NOW I SWEAR I DON'T KNOW WHY

(As MONA *begins the last verse the following takes place:*

>*The* GIRLS *move across the stage slowly with suitcases making a line behind* MONA, *expressionless.*

>*A strange slow motion scene takes place on the balcony. The* GOVERNOR'S AIDE *presents the* GOVERNOR. *The* SENATOR *applauds the* GOVERNOR. MELVIN *comes out beaming and the* GOVERNOR *awards him a plaque for meritorious service, preserving the morals of the great state of Texas.*

>*There is a freeze, as if a picture was snapped. Then* MONA *sings the last line in spotlight.)*

MISS MONA. (*Continued.*)
GUESS LIFE'S A ONE WAY TICKET TO NOWHERE
GOD, WISH I WAS TRAVELIN' FREE . . .
ONCE I HAD A
ONE WAY TICKET TO GO WHERE
ANYTHING WAS POSSIBLE FOR ME.
ANYTHING WAS POSSIBLE FOR ME.

(*The curtain call should be a big hoedown finale. Get the people stomping and clapping.*)

PROPS: STAGE LEFT

ACT I:

billfold with money
check (need new check each performance)
handcane
wheelchair (water in ash tray)
cigarettes (light)
lighter
dust rag
five flashlights (plus two as extras)
sheet music
working microphone on stand (preset: leet port #one) for
    watchdog
nine cue cards
Jewel's overnight bag
five white decorations
two red decorations
two bouquets of flowers
t.v. camera
headphones
working shotgun microphone
tape recorder
coke can with water
pie case with two pie slices
round bentwood table
two bentwood chairs
newspaper
three dolls (chambers, merchant, king)
bench with three lonestar beer cans
hamper
ledger with pen
eyeglasses
extra blank gun

Act II:

ten flags
long flashlight
three suitcases: (Linda Lou, Durla, Ginger)
deck of playing cards
award plaque
rope for twirling

PROPS: STAGE RIGHT

ACT I:
paper money
chicken with chicken bag
five flashlights (plus two for replacements)
nail file
two bouquets of flowers
long flashlight (plus extra)
working microphone on stand (preset: right port #one)
extra cable with attachment for Thorpe's microphone
sheet music
whistle
three dolls (zalkind, brown, gelke)
three pads, pens, pencils.

ACT II:
Sheriff's breakfast: two fried eggs, coffee cup with water,
                    biscuits, fork & knife, napkin, salt, tray.
tinfoil to cover tray
rolling chair
telephone
four suitcases
one canvas bag
wheelchair

COSTUME PLOT

TWENTY FANS
    six choir robes
    THREE COWBOYS jeans, shirts, bandannas
    SHY KID longjohns, shirt, pants
    FARMER underwear, shirt, overalls
    TRAVELING SALESMAN suit, shirt, bow tie, straw hat
    SLICK DUDE jeans, jeansjacket, shirt, bandanna
    MISS WULLA JEAN dress, jewels
    PUSHER (lady who pushes wheelchair) pants and top
    one piano shawl
    one thirtys dress
    one teddy with jacket
    one bra, top pants with robe
PISSANT
    MONA white pants, fringed top jacket, gold shoes
    JEWEL house dress, apron, boots
    eight girls . . ass't
    SHY old skirt, top, jacket, boots
    ANGEL white boots, white dress, pink undies
GIRL YOU'RE A WOMAN
    SHY sequin dress, undershirt, white panties
    GINGER leopard jumpsuit
WATCHDOG
    MELVIN P. THORPE dressy light blue suit, flag tie, white shirt,
        blue, red and white boots, white belt, two holsters
    SIX DOGETTES six gold jackets, six blue pants, six blue ties,
        six white shirts, six belts, six grey hats
    FOUR LADIES four yellow floor length dresses, four pair shoes
TWENTY FOUR HOURS
    JEWEL two piece black outfit, shoes
    ten ladies ass't outfits
    ANGEL pink quilted robe
SHERIFF OFFICE
    SHERIFF pants, shirt, jacket, belt, boots, hat, gunbelt, string
        tie, badge.
CAFE SCENE
    C. J. SCRUGGS red pants and sox, white shirt, shoes, striped
        tie, loud jacket

MAYOR brown suit, green shirt, tie, brown shoes and sox, straw hat.

EDSEL seersucker suit, blue shirt, tie, black shoes and sox

DOATSEY waitress uniform, white shoes, gingham hat and apron

ANGELETTES

six of each: shirt, bra, vest, cuffs, boots, scarves, hats with wigs

CHIP BREWSTER dark shoes, pants, hat, raincoat

AGGIES

eight of each: boots, white pants, jerseys, plaid shirts, belts, white scarves helmets, hats.

SENATOR hat, white shirt, tie, grey western suit, black boots

PROM

ten prom gowns with accessories and flat shoes

MONA blue strapless dress, silver shoes.

FOUR PHOTOGRAPHERS . . . four hats, four coats

SIDESTEP

Gov. pinstriped suit, white shirt, navy tie, grey hat, boots, belt

FEMALE REPORTER beige skirt, blouse, shoes

THREE MALE REPORTERS pants, shirts, jackets

Gov. AIDE beige suit, vest, white shirt, tie

NO LIES

ten cocktail dresses

MONA black sequin dress

JEWEL black skirt, flower blouse

GOOD OLD GIRL

eight of each: jeans, shirts, bandannas

HARD CANDY

ten ladies go away outfits, boots, hats

MONA pants, red shirt, belt, boots

JEWEL pants, blouse

BAND

Nine shirts, six red, three black

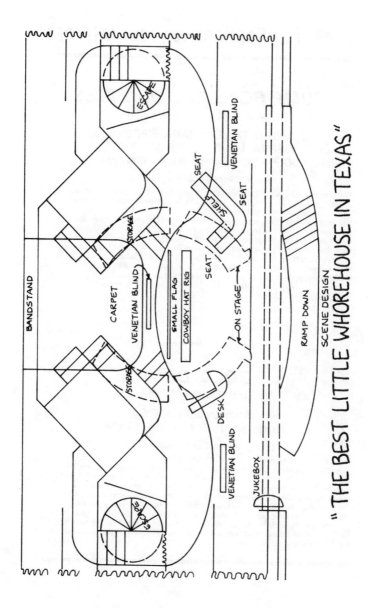

" THE BEST LITTLE WHOREHOUSE IN TEXAS"

SCENE DESIGN

Other Publications for Your Interest

PUMP BOYS AND DINETTES

(ALL GROUPS—MUSICAL)

By JOHN FOLEY, MARK HARDWICK, DEBRA MONK, CASS MORGAN, JOHN SCHIMMEL and JIM WANN

4 men, 2 women—Composite interior

This delightful little show went from Off Off Broadway to Off Broadway to Broadway, where it had a long run. This is an evening of country/western songs performed by the actors—on guitars, piano, bass and, yes, kitchen utensils. There are the four Pump Boys: L.M. on the Piano (singing such delights as "The Night Dolly Parton Was Almost Mine"), Jim on rhythm guitar (the spokesman of the Pump Boys), Jackson on lead guitar (whose rocker about Mona, a check-out girl at Woolworth's, stops the show) and Eddie, who plays bass. The Dinettes are Prudie and Rhetta Cupp, who run the Double Cupp Diner across from the Pump Boys' gas station. "Totally delightful . . . the easiest, chummiest, happiest show in town."—Newsweek. "Totally terrific."—N.Y. Post. "It tickles the funny bone and makes everybody feel, just for the evening, like a good ole boy or a good ole girl."—Time. "It doesn't merely celebrate the value of friendship and life's simple pleasures, it embodies them."—N.Y. Times. (#18135)

GOLD DUST

(ALL GROUPS—MUSICAL)

Book by JON JORY
Music and Lyrics by JIM WANN

5 men, 3 women, 3 piece combo—Interior

Set in a saloon in a western mining camp in the 1850's, *Gold Dust* is a very loose musical adaptation of Molière's *The Miser*. The story concerns a prospector named Jebediah Harp who has hit it rich and hoards his gold. Perfect for high schools, colleges and community theatres, this is another hit from Louisville's famed Actors Theater. The music and lyrics are by the very talented Jim Wann, whose other works include *Pump Boys and Dinettes*, *Diamond Studs* and *Hot Grog*. "It's spunky and raucous, clangorous and tuneful. It overflows with a theatrical zest that is pretty much irresistible."—Louisville Courier Journal. ". . . the small musical that budget-minded theatres across the land have been praying for."—Louisville Times. "Best of all is Wann's music, a mixture of jazz, blues, rock, folk and country-western styles."—Variety. (#9134)

Other Publications for Your Interest

A . . . MY NAME IS ALICE
(LITTLE THEATRE—REVUE)

Conceived by JOAN MICKLIN SILVER
and JULIANNE BOYD

5 women—Bare stage with set pieces

This terrific new show definitely rates an "A"—in fact, an "A-*plus*"! Originally produced by the Women's Project at the American Place Theatre in New York City, "Alice" settled down for a long run at the Village Gate, off Broadway. When you hear the songs, and read the sketches, you'll know why. The music runs the gamut from blues to torch to rock to wistful easy listening. There are hilarious songs, such as "Honeypot" (about a Black blues singer who can only sing about sex euphemistically) and heartbreakingly beautiful numbers such as "I Sure Like the Boys". A . . . *My Name is Alice* is a feminist revue in the best sense. It could charm even the most die-hard male chauvinist. "Delightful . . . the music and lyrics are so sophisticated that they can carry the weight of one-act plays".—NY Times. "Bright, party-time, pick-me-up stuff . . . Bouncy music, witty patter, and a bundle of laughs".—NY Post. (#3647)

I'M GETTING MY ACT TOGETHER AND TAKING IT ON THE ROAD
(ALL GROUPS—MUSICAL)

Book and Lyrics by GRETCHEN CRYER
Music by NANCY FORD

6 men, 4 women—Bare stage

This new musical by the authors of *The Last Sweet Days of Isaac* was a hit at Joseph Papp's Public Theatre and transferred to the Circle-in-the-Square theatre in New York for a successful off-Broadway run. It is about a 40-year-old song writer who wants to make a come-back. The central conflict is between the song writer and her manager. She wants to include feminist material in her act—he wants her to go back to the syrupy-sweet, non-controversial formula which was once successful. "Clearly the most imaginative and melodic score heard in New York all season."—Soho Weekly News. "Brash, funny, very agreeable in its brash and funny way, and moreover, it touches a special emotional chord for our times."—N.Y. Post. (#11025)

ᘓᘓᘓᘓᘓᘓᘓᘓᘓᘓᘓᘓᘓᘓᘓᘓᘓᘓᘓᘓᘓᘓᘓᘓ

ON THE TWENTIETH CENTURY
(ALL GROUPS—MUSICAL COMEDY)

Book and Lyrics by ADOLPH GREEN and
BETTY COMDEN, Music by CY COLEMAN

17 principal roles, plus singers and extras (doubling possible)—Various sets

Whether performed with elaborate scenery, or on a simple skeletal scale, this brilliantly comic musical can appeal to audiences everywhere. This is truly an extravagant show—but its extravagance lies not in its scenery and physical production, but in the boisterous, tumultuous energy—and in the lush and sprightly energetic surge of its very melodic score. The story concerns the efforts of a flamboyant theatrical impressario to persuade a film star to appear in his next production, to outwit rival producers and creditors, to rid himself of religious nut Letitia Primrose (played by Imogene Coca on Broadway) and Lily's film star boyfriend Bruce Granit (who's as strong in profile as he is weak in brains). And, he must do all this before the famed 20th Century Ltd. reaches NYC! The story, and it's two leading characters—the mad impressario Oscar Jaffe and the love of his life and his greatest star Lily Garland—can be loved and enjoyed by all audiences. "Spectacular . . . funny . . . elegant . . . civilized wit and wild humor."—N.Y. Times. "A perfect musical . . . a gorgeous show!"—N.Y. Post.   (#819)

KURT VONNEGUT'S
GOD BLESS YOU,
MR. ROSEWATER
(MUSICAL SATIRE)

By the creators of
LITTLE SHOP OF HORRORS

Book and Lyrics by HOWARD ASHMAN
Music by ALAN MENKEN
Additional lyrics by DENNIS GREEN

**10 men, 4 women (principals—also double smaller roles),
extras, musicians—Various interiors and exteriors**

"One of Vonnegut's most affecting and likeable novels becomes an affecting and likable theatrical experience, with more inventiveness, cockeyed characters, high-muzzle-velocity dialogue and just plain energy that you get from the majority of play-wrights."—Newsweek. Eliot Rosewater's a well-intentioned idealist and philanthropic nut—and as president of a multi-million family foundation dispenses money to arcane and artsy-crafty projects. He's also a World War II veteran with a guilt complex, haunted by all this wealth—and also slightly crazy. His outlandish behavior enrages his senator dad, alienates his society-conscious wife—and the money attracts a young, shyster lawyer who tries to divert it to an obscure branch of the family. It portrays Vonnegut's vision of money, avarice and human behavior—as it aims a satrical fusillade at plastic America, fast foods, trademarks, slogans, media blitzes and the follies of materialism. "A charming, delightful, unexpected and thoughtful musical."—N.Y. Post.   (#630)

ᘓᘓᘓᘓᘓᘓᘓᘓᘓᘓᘓᘓᘓᘓᘓᘓᘓᘓᘓᘓᘓᘓᘓ